P9-CBI-983

Bret Harte

Twayne's United States Authors Series

David J. Nordloh, Editor

Indiana University

TUSAS 600

BRET HARTE

Bret Harte

Gary Scharnhorst

University of New Mexico

Twayne Publishers • New York
Maxwell Macmillan Canada • Toronto
Maxwell Macmillan International • New York   Oxford   Singapore   Sydney

Bret Harte
Gary Scharnhorst

Copyright 1992 by Twayne Publishers.

Twayne Publishers
Macmillan Publishing Company
866 Third Avenue
New York, New York 10022

Maxwell Macmillan Canada Inc.
1200 Eglinton Avenue East
Suite 200
Don Mills, Ontario M3C 3N1

Macmillan Publishing Company is a member of the Maxwell Communication Group of Companies.

10 9 8 7 6 5 4 3 2 1

The paper used in this publication meets the minimum requirements of American National Standard for Information Sciences—Permanence of Paper for Printed Library Materials, ANSI Z39.48-1984. ∞™

Printed and bound in the United States of America.

Library of Congress Cataloging-in-Publication Data

Scharnhorst, Gary.
     Bret Harte / Gary Scharnhorst.
          p.   cm. — (Twayne's United States authors series : TUSAS 600)
     Includes bibliographical references and index.
     ISBN 0-8057-7648-6 (alk. paper)
     1. Harte, Bret, 1836–1902 — Criticism and interpretation.
     2. Western stories — History and criticism.   I. Title.   II. Series.
     PS1834.S33   1992
     813'.4 — dc20   91-45870
                                                                          CIP

To my friends at Scalo,
where much of this book was written.

Contents

Preface

He was a supernova in the literary firmament, a bright Western star quickly faded, or so goes the conventional estimate of his career. Bret Harte was, in 1871, the best-paid and arguably the most popular writer in America. A pioneer in the use of California local color in his fiction, Harte had enjoyed a long literary apprenticeship on the West Coast, first as a newspaperman and patriotic poet, then as a storyteller and editor of the *Overland Monthly*. His story "The Luck of Roaring Camp," published without signature in the second issue of the magazine, became an immediate sensation. "It reached across the continent and startled the Academists on the Atlantic Coast," as Kate Chopin recalled later.[1] His was a new voice in American fiction, and his subject was remarkably fresh: California during the Gold Rush, a veritable melting pot of Native Americans, Eastern miners and gamblers, Chinese immigrants, and Hispanics. Harte's best stories were set in the mining country or near it in boomtowns such as Sacramento and San Francisco during the 1850s, a place and moment in history he remembered from his boyhood.

Lured by the promise of literary success, Harte traveled across the continent to Boston in 1871, a trip W. D. Howells later compared to "the progress of a prince" in the "universal attention and interest" it attracted (*LFA, 290*). Removed from the West and the sources of his inspiration, however, Harte soon exhausted both his welcome and the rich vein of material he had been working. As one wit wisecracked at the time, he "reversed the path of the sun. He rose splendidly in the West and set in darkness in the East."[2] Although he would collaborate on a play with no less a luminary than Mark Twain in 1877, he left America for Europe, never to return, the next year. Most of his later tales merely follow the same standard formula. "I grind out the old tunes on the old organ and gather up the coppers," he ruefully admitted in 1879 (*L, 154*). More than any other American writer of his generation, Bret Harte became a creature of the marketplace, a major minor writer ruined by his early and too-sudden success.

Still, Harte's fiction may be defended in much the same way that Twain praised Wagner's music: it "isn't as bad as it sounds." What Harte wrote in "Tennessee's Partner" of the gulches and barrooms of

Sandy Bar is, in fact, equally true of his fiction as a whole: there "all
sentiment was modified by a strong sense of humor" (VII, 57). His
stories were, like the halcyon days Jack Hamlin recollects in *Gabriel
Conroy,* "an ingenious combination of the sentimental and the humorous" (*GC* II, 34). Although his work is now neglected, Harte was a
respected man of letters among his contemporaries, and his best stories
merited their reputation and popularity. "Waves of influence run from
the man," Henry Seidel Canby wrote in 1926, "and indeed the literary
West may be said to have founded itself upon the imagination of Bret
Harte."[3] His career, in fact, broadly paralleled Twain's: both men began as Western journalists, turned to humor and platform speaking,
and became literary expatriates and erstwhile social satirists. "Though
I am generally placed at the head of my breed of scribblers in this part
of the country," Twain wrote his family from San Francisco in January
1866, "the place properly belongs to Bret Harte" (*MTL* I, 328). He
reiterated the point almost three years later in a letter to Jervis Lang-
don: Harte, he claimed, is "the finest writer" in the West (*MTL* II,
359). Before their estrangement, Twain allowed that Harte, his former
editor, "trimmed and trained and schooled me patiently until he
changed me from an awkward utterer of coarse grotesquenesses to a
writer of paragraphs and chapters that have found a certain favor."[4]
However minor his art or modest his achievement, moreover, Harte
should be remembered as the prototype of the modern man of letters
as a man of business. For better or worse, he commercialized the role
of the writer in post–Civil War America.

His biography is nothing less than a study in vaulting ambition and
unrealized promise. Harte willingly accommodated the economic order
that calculated royalties on the basis of sales (and implicitly profits),
but he repeatedly quarreled with publishers, producers, and managers
whose interests were, after all, never quite identical with his own. He
was haunted to the end of his life by the specter of the hardscrabble
winter of 1877–78, when he and his family lived literally hand-to-
mouth. Afterwards the demands on his income only increased: though
he resided out of the country and away from his family for almost 25
years, he continued to support them, mostly by his writing. By then
less a craftsman than a literary celebrity who traded on his name, he
gauged the market for his work with a calculating eye and, as Howells
put it, "wrote Bret Harte over and over again as long as he lived" (*LFA,*
299). Like the Writer of Stories he depicted in "A Romance of the
Line" (1900), Harte was never at a loss "for material,—his subjects

were usually the same" (X, 259). He privately disparaged these "monotonous romances" with their gamblers and rustic miners (L, 299). Despite the depreciation of his note, he continued to work regularly as a magazinist until his death in 1902.

In this volume, I eschew the piecemeal treatment usually accorded Harte in favor of a comprehensive approach. Rather than focus on only one or two aspects of his work, I will discuss his early successes as a regionalist, his literary criticism, his major short stories, his lectures, his poetry and drama, and his late fiction. For reasons that will be obvious, I emphasize the early years of his career. Parenthetically, I should note the pressing need for a new and reliable edition of Harte's letters and for a complete bibliography of his works that lists all first appearances of his poems and stories, especially those late pieces written for syndication, in U.S. and British periodicals.

I am grateful to the National Endowment for the Humanities and the Resource Allocations Committee at the University of New Mexico for the generous support of my research on this book; to Lynda Fuller–Clendenning of the Alderman Library at the University of Virginia and Ray Wemmlinger of the Hampden–Booth Theatre Library in New York for their help during my visits; and to John and Mary Miller, Mary Bess Whidden, George Arms, Paul Hadella, Charles Johanningsmeier, and my cousin Lisa (with an "s") for assisting me with some biographical and bibliographical details. I also wish to acknowledge the cooperation of librarians at the following institutions, all of whom supplied me with copies of Harte's letters and granted me the requisite permissions to cite them in these pages: Bancroft Library, University of California, Berkeley; Olin Library, Cornell University; Rutherford B. Hayes Presidential Center; Hampden-Booth Theatre Library; Houghton Library, Harvard University; Huntington Library; Lilly Library, Indiana University; Knox College Library; Library of Congress; Morristown Historical National Park; Massachusetts Historical Society; Minnesota Historical Society; Princeton University Library; San Francisco Public Library; Research Library, University of California at Los Angeles; Alderman Library, University of Virginia; Olin Memorial Library, Wesleyan University; and Beinecke Library, Yale University.

Chronology

and "The Idyl of Red Gulch" in December. Each of these stories appears in the *Overland Monthly*.

1870   Publishes "Brown of Calaveras" in March and the poem "Plain Language from Truthful James" in September, both appearing in the *Overland Monthly*. Publishes *The Luck of Roaring Camp and Other Stories*. Declines appointment as Professor of Recent Literature at the new University of California, Berkeley.

1871   Leaves San Francisco with his family 2 February. Contracts with Fields, Osgood & Co. 6 March to contribute exclusively to the *Atlantic Monthly* and *Every Saturday* for 12 months for $10,000. Delivers Phi Beta Kappa poem at Harvard University commencement in June.

1871–1878   Resides in the East with his family.

1872   Publishes "How Santa Claus Came to Simpson's Bar" in the *Atlantic Monthly* in March.

1872–1875   Lectures on "The Argonauts of '49" and "American Humor" throughout the eastern and southern U.S.

1876   *Gabriel Conroy*. His play *Two Men of Sandy Bar* is produced at the Union Square Theatre in New York during August and September.

1877   The play *Ah Sin,* written with Mark Twain, is produced at Fifth Avenue Theatre in New York during July and August.

1878–1880   Commercial agent of the U.S. in Crefeld, Prussia.

1880–1885   U.S. Consul in Glasgow, Scotland.

1884   Contracts with A. P. Watt, literary agent, to handle his business affairs.

1885   Moves into the home of Arthur Van de Velde, chancellor of the Belgian Legation in London.

1887   Publishes *The Crusade of the Excelsior.*

1889   Publishes "A Waif of the Plains," "An Ingénue of the Sierras," and "A Protégée of Jack Hamlin's."

1893   Publishes "Susy."

1895   Publishes "Clarence."

1896 The play *Sue*, written with T. Edgar Pemberton, is produced at Hoyt's Theatre in New York and the Museum Theatre in Boston during September through December.

1897 Publishes "The Ancestors of Peter Atherly."

1898 *Sue* produced at the Garrick Theatre in London during June and July.

1899 Publishes "Mr. Jack Hamlin's Mediation."

1902 Dies on 5 May of cancer of the throat in Camberley, Surrey.

Chapter One
Literary Apprenticeship

"To the best of my knowledge and beliefs I was born in Albany, N.Y. on the 25th day of August, 1839," Bret Harte once replied to an inquiry.[1] Like so many of his autobiographical statements, however, this one stands in uneasy relation to the facts: Harte correctly identified his place of birth, but he shaved three years off his age. To the end of his life he concealed his "Jewish birth"—he was the grandson of Bernard Hart, an orthodox Jew—"as carefully as if he considered it a disgrace," or so Mark Twain maintained (*MT–HL* I, 235). In an 1893 interview Harte claimed that, at the tender age of 12, he had run away "from school and home and crossed the plains with a caravan to California," later modeling the opening chapters of his story "A Waif of the Plains" upon his "actual experience" (Haskell, 17). The truth is, unfortunately, far more prosaic. As George Stewart has explained in painstaking detail, Harte immigrated to California in 1854 by ocean steamer to rejoin his widowed mother, who had married a prosperous Oakland politician (Stewart, 29–33). Similarly, Harte would aver in "How I Went to the Mines" (1899) that he had dug for gold in the foothills of Tuolumne County for several weeks in 1855 (IX, 335–55). In fact, as Patrick Morrow concluded, he probably "spent less time in the Mother Lode than many of today's enthusiastic tourists."[2] The Western mythology that accreted about Harte, as in the case of Whitman's bohemian reputation, was in no small part a product of the writer's own gift for self-promotion. He told an interviewer in 1894 that he had been a guard on a Wells Fargo stagecoach "for some months" after leaving the mine fields and that both his predecessor and his successor in the job were shot by highwaymen (Dam, 41–42). Yet, as Stewart has tactfully noted, the "sentence does not check with other information" (Stewart, 57). In truth, Harte mostly earned his living as a young man by teaching, although he was briefly employed as a pharmacist's assistant and, for a few weeks in 1857, as a Wells Fargo courier. Harte asserted in the same interview that he had "never in my life had an article refused publication" (Dam, 42). Yet in March 1879, at the nadir of his literary career, he had complained in a letter to his wife Anna that, "They are not paying me well for my articles in America—nor do they seem to care much for them. The *Atlantic* don't want anything, and *Scribner* has taken only one."[3] Why would Harte swear publicly he had never had a manuscript rejected? He hinted at an explanation in another letter to Anna in September 1885: "I must not try to *force* the market for my work, for the sake of momentary gain, and I must not let the publishers think I am getting anxious."[4] For the record, both of these letters are omitted from the sanitized *The Letters of Bret Harte* compiled by his grandson.

"I am fit for nothing else"

Judging from all available evidence, Harte's literary ambitions were formed early. His father, Henry Hart, had been a teacher—the son would later describe him as "a tutor of Greek"—at the Ellington Institute and other private academies in upstate New York. As a child, young Francis Brett Harte read such books as "Froissart's 'Chronicles of the Middle Ages,' 'Don Quixote,' [and] the story of the Argonauts," which he found on his father's shelves (Dam, 40). According to family tradition, he was reading Shakespeare at six, Dickens at seven, and Montaigne at nine.[5] Harte often insisted in later years that he had published his first poem at age 11 in the *New York Sunday Atlas,* though this work has so far eluded bibliographers. In any event, much as Louisa May Alcott and Horatio Alger, Jr., wrote at about the same time for such Boston literary weeklies as *The Flag of Our Union,* Harte began to contribute bits of verse and travel essays to a San Francisco weekly, the *Golden Era,* in 1857, and he published a crude ballad entitled "Dolores" in the *Knickerbocker* in January 1858. He was, at the time, barely 21 years old. According to a diary he kept while working as a tutor in the home of a rancher in Humboldt County, near Uniontown, California, between October 1857 and March 1858, Harte wrote stories and poems in his spare time; read widely, including Dickens' *Barnaby Rudge,* Irving's *Life of Washington,* and Prescott's *The Conquest of Peru*; and taught a young neighbor girl to read. He also resolved during these months to pursue a literary career, lured by the fame and fortune such a career seemed to offer. As he noted in his diary for 31 December 1857,

I am—at the commencement of this year—a teacher at a salary of $25 per mo. Last year at this time I was unemployed. . . . I have taught school, played the Expressman for a brief delightful hour and have travelled some. I have added to my slight stock of experiences and have suffered considerable. Ah! well did the cynical Walpole say life is a comedy to them who think—a tragedy to them who feel.—I both think and feel. My life is a mixture of broad caricature and farce when I think of others, it is a melodrama when I feel for myself. In these 365 days I have again put forth a feeble essay toward fame and perhaps fortune—I have tried literature albeit in an humble way—successfully—I have written some pretty passable verse and some prose (good) which have been published. The conviction forced on me by observation and not by vain enthusiasm [is] that I am fit for nothing else. . . . Perhaps I may succeed—if not I can at least make the trial. Therefore I consecrate this year or as much as God may grant for my service—to honest heartfelt sincere labor and devotion to this occupation.—God help me—may I succeed.[6]

This paragraph is all the more remarkable because it appears in one of the earliest extant documents from Harte's pen, located today in the Bancroft Library at the University of California at Berkeley.

Within a year he was employed by the *Northern Californian,* a weekly newspaper published at Uniontown, as a so-called printer's devil or compositor's assistant. To paraphrase Melville, the printing press was his Harvard and his Yale. Harte composed sketches and poems for the paper quite literally while typesetting its columns. "I was very young when I first began to write for the press," he recalled years later. "I learned to combine the composition of the editorial with the setting of its type" and in order "to save my fingers mechanical drudgery some-what condensed my style."[7] He soon became a junior editor of sorts, entrusted with the operation of the paper during the editor's absences. Thus Harte was in charge of the *Northern Californian* in late February 1860 when several white vigilantes massacred more than 60 Indians, most of them women and children, near Eureka. In some of his earlier sketches, Harte had written derisively of the "Diggers." On a visit to the Mad River village in December 1857 he had watched "some old squaws drying salmon."[8] In his account of this excursion for the *Golden Era* he described one of these women, whom he named "Rat Eyed Sal," in horrifying detail: her "native ugliness" was compounded by small-pox scars, he wrote. When she smiled, "her teeth reminded one painfully of the moss-covered stones in some country churchyard." Moreover, "the cartilage of her nose was gone and the eyelids eaten from the co[r]nea." Inside her hut, Harte saw a child, "a harmless specimen of the half-breed—a mere cub—the rogue in swaddling clothes—the thief embryo—the incipient scamp."[9] The following Feb-ruary, however, Harte headlined the news from Eureka "Indiscriminate

Massacre of Indians / Women and Children Butchered," blamed the slaughter on the advocates of Indian extermination, and appealed to local settlers to commiserate with the victims' families. In an outraged editorial, he pictured the mutilated bodies: "Old Women wrinkled and decripit lay weltering in blood, their brains dashed out and dabbled with their long grey hair. Infants scarce a span long, with their faces cloven with hatchets and their bodies ghastly with wounds."[10] Within the month, apparently under threat to his life, Harte quit his job and abruptly left Uniontown for sanctuary in San Francisco. Over the next few years, however, his portrayals of Indians and mixed-bloods like little Tommy Luck and Jack Hamlin (a.k.a. Comanche Jack), while not altogether free of the stereotypical, were markedly sympathetic.

Despite the inauspicious circumstances of his move to the bay, he soon prospered there. Some 40 years later, in "Bohemian Days in San Francisco," Harte would recall how upon his arrival he had strolled along the City Front on "steamer night," the evening before the departure of the mail ship for the "States," and wandered through the Spanish Quarter "where three centuries of quaint customs, speech, and dress were still preserved, where the proverbs of Sancho Panza were still spoken in the language of Cervantes" (X, 305). After "an idle week, spent in listless outlook for employment" (X, 302), he went to work for the *Golden Era,* the weekly that had printed his early poems and essays. As in Uniontown, he was a compositor in two senses of the term: he both set type and contributed to its pages. In fact, his first published fiction—the first piece he signed with the pen name "Bret Harte"—appeared in the 29 April 1860 issue, barely a month after his arrival in the city. "My Metamorphosis" is the rather limp story of a young itinerant artist named Van Daub who, surprised while bathing in a "sylvan lake," impersonates a statue with "a sort of fig-leaf apron" (Kozlay, 3–11). It betrays "the schoolboy's inability to make a story out of a situation," as Stewart concludes (Stewart, 99). As if to prove the point, Harte developed the same premise in one of the last of his stories, "A Vision of the Fountain" (1900), which is more practiced though no less formulaic. Both versions end, for example, as the hero proposes marriage to the fair lady who interrupted his swim.

Harte wrote literally dozens of poems, stories, and sketches for the *Golden Era* over the next three years, many of them under the pseudonym "the Bohemian." He would subsequently collect several of these pieces (e.g., "Mission Dolores," "The Man of No Account," "High-Water Mark") in *The Luck of Roaring Camp and Other Sketches* (1870), his most important single book. However, the most ambitious of his early writings to merit inclusion in this volume—and, eventually, in his collected works—is the novella "The Work on Red Mountain," published serially in the *Golden Era* in December 1860. Although still only 24 years old, Harte was already hitting his stride in this tale, set in the fictional mining town of Smith's Pocket in central California. The story is also semiautobiographic: the major characters, an unnamed teacher and his pupil Melissa (or M'liss) Smith, are apparently modeled upon Harte and the young girl he had taught to read during his months as tutor in Humboldt County. M'liss, the motherless child of Old Bummer Smith, the prospector who discovered the gold which gave the town its name, is "an incorrigible girl" of "lawless character," a "dirty and shabbily clad" ragamuffin (VII, 144). Margaret Duckett fairly compares "the shabby little M'liss" to Huck Finn (Duckett 1964, 329). Both children of nature are precocious and intuitively wise beyond their years. M'liss is also harried and oppressed by the agents of "civilization," particularly the Reverend Mr. McSnagley, who compels her to attend his Sunday school and prays for her conversion. On her part, M'liss willingly attends the school kept by the "master" and lives with the Morphers, a family of kind but bumbling fools. Clytemnestra Morpher, age 15 and something of a Sid Sawyer type, was, according to Harte, "the realization of her mother's immaculate conception,— neat, orderly, and dull" (VII, 156). The schoolmaster, who is renamed Mr. Gray, significantly enough, in Harte's 1863 revision of the story, is figuratively torn between the fair Clytie and "the very dark brunette" M'liss (VII, 167)—between, that is, the domesticity and independence they respectively represent. In the original version, the teacher recognizes the impropriety of his "foolish, romantic, and unpractical" feeling for M'liss (VII, 168), but when a rounder accuses him of nymphomania—"Want her yourself, do you? That cock won't fight here, young man!"—he responds not with a denial but by guiltily striking "the brute full in his grinning face" (VII, 179). This version of the story ends as the schoolmaster, having rescued M'liss from "an existence worse than death" (VII, 178), walks out of the town hand-in-hand with his ward.

The popularity of "The Work on Red Mountain" prompted Harte, at the suggestion of the owner of the *Golden Era,* to revise it three years later. This later version, more than twice the length of the original, appeared in 10 installments of the paper between September and December 1863 as "The Story of M'liss." Harte finally "wound it up in disgust," as he later wrote James R. Osgood, and afterward he "always preferred [his] first conception" to the second one, with its byzantine subplots about lost gold mines and the murder of Old Bummer Smith (*L*, 23). Harte's comment was an astute one. Whereas the original version resolves the conflict between the domestic and the natural virtues in M'liss's favor, the revision is simply ambiguous. M'liss helps her father's killer—now insane—escape from jail, an action Harte implicitly condones. By taking justice into her own hands, however, she prevents a lynch mob from hanging the criminal; that is, her act, while lawless, deters lawlessness. Harte in effect suggests that frontier types such as M'liss can be both savage and gentle. Little wonder that Harte depicted gamblers and prostitutes as outlaws with hearts of gold in such later stories as "The Outcasts of Poker Flat" and "Miggles." Such characters do not so much incarnate as obscure the conflict between freedom and order. In the end, the 1863 "M'liss" breaks off rather than concludes. M'liss's mother, a character Harte added in revision, flirts with Mr. Gray, but he fails to reciprocate her interest. A millionaire heiress, M'liss falls victim to the repressions of civilization. Under "her mother's protection and care" she begins to dress "more tastefully and neatly" and maintains "a guarded shyness totally different from her usual frank boldness. . . . There is a more strict attention to the conventionalities of life; her speech is more careful and guarded; her walk, literally, more womanly and graceful" (*Outcasts*, 95–96). In this version of the story, Harte's juvenile pariah does not "light out for the Territory ahead of the rest" but is adopted and "sivilized." M'liss is, in the final pages, indistinguishable from her rival Clytie Morpher. The conflict between the docile and the wild here is resolved in favor of the former. Unfortunately, the Signet paperback *The Outcasts of Poker Flat and Other Tales*, the most accessible modern edition of Harte's fiction, reprints only the latter version of the story.

In the summer of 1860, Harte's stories in the *Golden Era* attracted the attention of Jessie Benton Frémont, daughter of a U.S. Senator and wife of a military hero and former presidential candidate. Frémont took the fledgling writer under her wing and introduced him to her circle of influential friends, the clergyman Thomas Starr King chief among them. She later reminisced that Harte "settled into a regular visit" to her salon on Sunday and "for more than a year dined with us that day, bringing his manuscripts; astonished by the effect of some, at times huffed by less flattering opinion on others, but growing rapidly into larger perceptions." At Frémont's behest, he received a series of gov-

ernment appointments, first with the local office of the U.S. Surveyor
General, next with the U.S. Marshall in the state, then as secretary to
the Superintendent of the U.S. Branch Mint in San Francisco, a position he would fill until August 1869 at a monthly salary of $270
(Stewart, 140). These sinecures allowed Harte to quit his job with the
Golden Era and devote more of his time to writing. He was also able,
in August 1862, to marry the former Anna Griswold, a contralto in
the choir at Starr King's church. As Harte wrote Frémont at the time,
"If I were to be cast away on a desert island, I should expect a savage
to come forward with a three-cornered note from you to tell me that,
at your request, I had been appointed governor of the island at a salary
of two thousand four hundred dollars."[11] No longer a captive to the
columns of the *Golden Era,* he began to contribute to other San Francisco papers, including the *Daily Evening Bulletin* and, later, the *Californian,* a weekly literary paper he founded with Charles H. Webb in
the spring of 1864. Mark Twain, at the time a reporter for the *San
Francisco Call,* was an indirect beneficiary of Frémont's patronage when
Harte engaged him to write for the new paper. The *Golden Era* "wasn't
high-toned enough," Twain explained to his family back in Missouri,
but the *Californian* "circulates among the highest class of the community, & is the best literary paper in the United States" (*MTL* I,
312).

While Frémont was Harte's early sponsor, Starr King, minister of
the First Unitarian Church of San Francisco, became his first promoter.
King occasionally punctuated his public lectures with selections of
Harte's verse,[12] and he also negotiated Harte's original appearance in
the pages of the *Atlantic Monthly.* The former pastor of the Hollis Street
Church in Boston, King persuaded his friend James T. Fields, the editor of the *Atlantic Monthly,* to accept Harte's "The Legend of Monte
del Diablo" for publication. In January 1862, King mailed the manuscript of this Irvingesque story to Fields with a cover letter recom-
mending it:

Mr. F. B. Harte, a very bright young man who has been in literary ways for
a few years, has written a piece, wh[ich] I have not yet seen, but feel sure it
is good. He is a particular friend of Mrs. Jessie Frémont, who has a very high
opinion of his powers, & obtained for him a situation as clerk in the Land
Surveyor's office here. I shall read the piece before this note goes. I hope the
editors will accept it if it is worthy, for I am sure there is a great deal in
Harte, & an acceptance of his piece would inspirit him, & help literature on
this coast where we raise bigger trees & squashes than literati & brains.[13]

King also predicted in the fall of 1862 in a letter to the *Boston Transcript* that his young parishioner would "yet be known more widely in our literature."[14]

"The Legend of Monte del Diablo" appeared in the *Atlantic Monthly* for October 1863, in the same issue as Emerson's "Voluntaries" and Thoreau's "Life Without Principle." It recounts a "singular incident" that had occurred in California a century earlier: the pilgrimage of a devout priest to the summit of a mountain in the Sierras, where he envisions "a new Spain rising on these savage shores." Then the devil appears to him, as if in a dream, and pictures an alternative future for the West: "the declining glory of old Spain," the invasion of "pushing, bustling, panting, and swaggering Saxons" lured west by treasure. The Gold Rush is, it seems, Satan's scheme to "replace the Christian grace of holy Spain" with the infidelities of the blue eyes (XVII, 277–98). A reviewer for the *Boston Traveller* remarked that the story was "diabolically clever,"[15] and Stanley T. Williams and James C. Austin have described it more recently as "a distinguished story" and "a well-told tale."[16] Still, "The Legend of Monte del Diablo" was written on a subject uncharacteristic of Harte's best fiction. It was, in a sense, a false start. Despite Frémont's best efforts, she could not convince Fields to accept another of Harte's sketches. She peppered him with appeals and manuscripts until, late in 1863, Fields finally returned the submissions with a brief note: "Your young friend fails to interest. He is not piquant enough for the readers of the *Atlantic*."[17] Harte's work would not appear in the magazine again until 1871.

Civil War Poet

Although Harte later admitted he sometimes neglected Starr King's "heroic proportions" in the "familiar contemplation of his exquisite details" (Booth 1944, 133), he obviously admired the minister without stint or reservation as he would admire few other men. He paid eloquent tribute over the years to King's "broad, catholic spirit," his "liberal and broad humanity," his "flashing genius and personal magnetism" (*BHC*, 23, 56, 89). King had arrived in San Francisco in the spring of 1860 to establish a Unitarian beachhead on the Pacific coast, and during the Civil War he raised more than $1 million for the U.S. Sanitary Commission, a prototype of the Red Cross. He was later commended in a resolution of the state legislature as "the man whose matchless oratory saved California for the Union."[18] On his part, Harte claimed, less ostentatiously, that King "infused into this hard money-loving community something of his own tenderness and magnanimity" and "cheated the people into the belief that they were generous" (*BHC*, 119). With such Black Republican friends as King and Frémont, at any rate, Harte enlisted in the Union cause, though not literally in its armies, even before the first shots were fired at Fort Sumter. During the war he wrote more than 40 patriotic poems on subjects such as charity fairs, California copperheads, and the battles of Gettysburg and Malvern Hill. Ironically, only one of them, "The Copperhead," even mentions slavery, comparing the coil of the serpent in "the ooze and the drip" of the swamp to the "slave-driver's whip" (VIII, 20). The peculiar institution was, quite simply, not a burning issue on the West Coast. Harte was "chiefly a vigorous laureate for a patriotic day," Joseph B. Harrison has observed, and his lyrics, with their martial meter and solemn tone, are as a group structurally similar to Whitman's *Drum Taps*: ". . . they begin with battle calls and go on to tales of field and home in war time, and these in turn lead to a song of reconciliation" (Harrison, xcii, xci).

"The Reveille," which King recited in the course of a patriotic rally in San Francisco in 1862, epitomizes the first of these forms:

> Hark! I hear the tramp of thousands,
>   And of armed men the hum;
> Lo! a nation's hosts have gathered
>   Round the quick alarming drum—
>   Saying "Come,
>   Freemen, come!
> Ere your heritage be wasted," said the quick alarming drum.

In the next three stanzas, Harte answers the objections of those who resist the call: first the economic ("Who shall stay and reap the harvest / When the autumn days shall come?"), next the political ("What if conquest—subjugation— / Even greater ills become?"), then the personal ("What if . . . When my brothers fall around me, / Should my heart grow cold and numb?"). The poem concludes on a note of reassurance. The cause of Union is a holy one, the war divinely sanctioned, and Americans are the new chosen people after all.

> Thus they answered—hoping, fearing,
>   Some in faith, and doubting some,
> Till a trumpet-voice proclaiming,
>   Said, "My chosen people, come!"

> Then the drum,
> Lo! was dumb,
> For the great heart of the nation, throbbing, answered,
> "Lord, we come!" (VIII, 10–11)

In retrospect, this call to arms seems unnecessary if not slightly ludicrous. Most of the 16,000 California enlistees were garrisoned within the state, and the conscription act passed by Congress in 1863 was simply not enforced on the Pacific Coast.[19]

Many of Harte's later Civil War poems are, as a result, marked by a certain defensiveness. As Jack Scherting explains, these works, whatever "their artistic defects, provide an inside approach to the problems and attitudes of Californians during the war."[20] Harte repeatedly insisted that, geographically separated from the rest of the Union, the western states should send money, not militia, to support the war effort. "Not ours," he wrote in "Our Privilege" (1862), "To meet the charge that treasure hurls / By sword and bayonet" or "to guide the fatal scythe." He assured his "brothers by the farther sea" that "still our faith is warm," that the "same red blood that dyes your fields / Here throbs in patriot pride." But if the West raises sufficient funds to support the Northern armies, then "Mercy's ringing gold shall chime / With Valor's clashing steel" (VIII, 12). He reiterated the point in the heroic couplets he composed in 1864 to commemorate the fourteenth anniversary of California's admission to the Union. In these lines he contrasted the battlefields of the East with the cornfields and relative peace of the West:

> There War's alarm the brazen trumpet rings—
> Here his love-song the mailed cicala sings;
> There bayonets glitter through the forest glades—
> Here yellow cornfields stack their peaceful blades;
> There the deep trench where Valor finds a grave—
> Here the long ditch that curbs the peaceful wave;
> There the bold sapper with his lighted train—
> Here the dark tunnel and its stores of gain;
> Here the full harvest and the wain's advance—
> There the Grim Reaper and the ambulance.

Again he admonished Easterners to "Judge not too idly that our toils are mean, / Though no new levies marshal on our green" because "ours the lot with peaceful, generous hand / To spread our bounty o'er the suffering land" (VIII, 33–35). As good as his word, he wrote several bombastic poems on behalf of these periodic campaigns for money. In "California to the Sanitary Commission" (1863), for example, he commended King and others for raising thousands of dollars for medical purposes and again intimated, especially in his pun on the word *draft,* that Californians were no less patriotic than other defenders of the Union:

> Our faith is the same,
> Though warmed in the sunshine, or tried in the flame;
> Would you say that we shrink, while your courage endures—
> That we offer our *draft* as an exchange for yours? (Kozlay, 362)

Harte fairly claimed later that California always gave money and its vote, if not its sons, to "the side of Union and republican principles," and that Starr King "had been cheered for ultra sentiments" at the beginning of the war, "which he would hardly have hazarded in any other city, not excepting Boston" (*BHC,* 82).

When Harte penned these words in 1866, King had been dead, the victim of a sudden attack of diphtheria, for nearly two years. His passing had inspired three of Harte's best-known poems, much as Lincoln's assassination spurred Whitman to devote an entire section of *Drum Taps* to memories of the late President. In "On a Pen of Thomas Starr King," Harte mourned the "unfinished strain," the cruelly interrupted melody of the "dead musician" (VIII, 16). In "At the Sepulchre," he compared Starr King to the crucified King of Kings around whose tomb "some of the humbler faith shall stand" and "watch its door," expecting "that some angel's hand / May roll the stone that lies before" (Kozlay, 311). And in "Relieving Guard," Harte testified in military metaphor to King's wartime defense of the Union. Whitman may well have borrowed his image of the "powerful western fallen star" in "When Lilacs Last in the Dooryard Bloom'd" from the second stanza of Harte's widely reprinted lyrical dialogue:

> Came the relief. "What, sentry, ho!
> How passed the night through thy long waking?"
> "Cold, cheerless, dark—as may befit
> The hour before the dawn is breaking."
>
> "No sight? no sound?" "No; nothing save
> The plover from the the marshes calling,

And in yon western sky, about
An hour ago, a star was falling."

"A star? There's nothing strange in that."
"No, nothing; but, above the thicket,
Somehow it seemed to me that God
Somewhere had just relieved a picket." (VIII, 13)

Harte would subsequently name his second son after King and dedicate
his first collection of fiction to King's memory.

"Best of the California Humorists"

The immediate postwar years were perhaps the most productive of
Harte's life. He was a frisky literary cub, if not yet a full-grown lion.
His first book, in fact, appeared shortly before Christmas 1865. A
collection of California verse entitled *Outcroppings,* it "contained beyond
the title page not one word of my own composition," as Harte reminisced in 1894 (XIX, 321). He had simply compiled the edition at the
request of Anton Roman, a prominent San Francisco bookseller. (Roman would found the *Overland Monthly* in 1869 and he would be the
exclusive West Coast agent for Mark Twain's *The Adventures of Tom
Sawyer* in 1876.) Harte owed his local reputation as a man of letters in
no small part to the controversy that dogged this anthology. After
Roman announced his plan to issue it, as Harte recalled, "I found
myself in daily and hourly receipt of sere and yellow fragments, originally torn from some dead and gone newspaper, creased and seamed
from long folding in wallet or pocketbook" (XIX, 323). He rejected
the "usual plagarisms" and "acrostics of patent medicines," and then
he began to winnow the remaining submissions with "sympathizing
concern" which proved to be "unappreciated by the rejected contributors" (XIX, 327). In the end, the volume contained only 42 pieces by
19 poets, of the approximately 1,300 "poet lariats" who submitted
their work.[21] Harte erred in his selections, if at all, on the side of the
conventional, mid-Victorian, and genteel.

Outcroppings was "a pretty little volume typographically, and exter-
nally a credit to pioneer book-making," as he remembered, and it was
instrumental in introducing the verse of such California writers as
Charles Warren Stoddard and Ina Coolbrith to the East. The collection
was lauded by William Cullen Bryant in the *New York Evening Post* and

N. P. Willis in the *Home Journal*.[22] Mark Twain opined that Harte had shown "rare good taste and ability in all respects save one—he has not put in a single line of his own poetry" (Stewart, 135). Harte also reviewed the book in the *Californian*, although, like Whitman under similar circumstances, he did not sign the notice. Then "the bolt fell," as he wrote later. Disappointed contributors became hostile critics. The Gold Hill, Nevada, *News*—which Harte caricatured later as "the Red Dog 'Jay Hawk'"—condemned the poetry as "purp-stuff" (XIX, 328), a phrase that still rankled him 30 years later. The *Alta California* derisively compared the lyrics to "nursery rhymes."[23] The *Oakland News* sniffed that the book proved "a man may be an author and no compiler," and the *San Francisco American Flag* dismissed *Outcroppings* as "beneath contempt,"[24] thereby earning Harte's disdain as "an incipient sort of New York Herald, plus its slang and slander" (*BHC,* 129). The *San Francisco Bulletin* declared that several of the selections "would be rejected by the editor of any well conducted newspaper."[25] Joseph Goodman, editor of the *Virginia City Territorial Enterprise* and one of the rejected poets, administered the coup de grace, branding Harte and Webb by name as "the little literary oligarchy of the *Californian*."[26] If such an oligarchy existed, ironically, Webb tried to resign from it. Even though he was one of the poets represented in the collection, he criticized it in newspaper columns on both coasts, though never over his own name, as mostly "trash," and he insinuated that Harte "threw in" a "number of verses" as "saps to the Cerberuses" in the West.[27] The *Bulletin* spread the most vitriolic of these notices across three columns of its 6 January 1866 issue "with the grim irony of exaggerated headlines," as Harte noted. The net effect of this publicity was that the book "sold tremendously" (XIX, 332), some 500 copies within its first six weeks in print.[28]

In all, however, the episode "showed Harte unpleasantly," as Stewart suggests; "for the first time he made public display of certain unadmirable qualities" (Stewart, 137). He was nearly sued by the person who had first proposed the project to Roman and who had made some initial selections. A month after the volume appeared, in the earliest of his letters published by his grandson in 1926, Harte asked Roman in New York to "relieve me of responsibility in the matter" (*L,* 3). In disavowing legal liability, however, he evaded the crux of the issue. As Stewart concludes, he should "have made sure of his moral right to use another's unprotected property" before beginning the work (Stewart, 138). In this same letter, Harte haggled with Roman over his remuneration: "I certainly cannot consent to any [payment] that is to be *contingent* upon the success of the volume," he protested. He had undertaken the edition for money, not because he believed the idea had merit: "If you will recall our interviews, you must remember that I was not sanguine of the success of this venture, and certainly did not base my ideas of payment on such contingency" (*L,* 4). He would repeatedly strike the same querulous tone with editors and publishers on both sides of the Atlantic to the end of his career. In this case, however, Harte had the last laugh: for "two months the most abused man on the Pacific slope," three years later he became "the editor of its first successful magazine" (XIX, 334) with Roman as his sponsor.

In the mid–1860s Harte also wrote a series of so-called condensed novels, travesties of works by such contemporary writers as Cooper, Dickens, Hugo, Charlotte Brontë, Wilkie Collins, T. S. Arthur, and Charles Reade. While these parodies often seem sophomoric today, they were extremely popular with nineteenth-century readers and spawned a host of imitations by such figures as Twain, Webb, and Frank Norris. The venerable *North American Review* described Harte as early as April 1866 as "a parodist of such genius that he seems a mirror into which novelists may look and be warned."[29] In "Muck-a-Muck: A Modern Indian Novel," for example, Harte both burlesqued Cooper's periphrastic style and ridiculed Natty Bumppo's marksmanship, particularly his rescue of Elizabeth Temple from a crouching panther in chapter 28 of *The Pioneers*:

The crack of a rifle rang through the woods. Three frightful yells were heard, and two sullen roars. Five animals bounded into the air and five lifeless bodies lay upon the plain. The well-aimed bullet had done its work. Entering the open throat of the grizzly, it had traversed his body only to enter the throat of the California lion, and in like manner the catamount, until it passed through into the respective foreheads of the bull and the buffalo, and finally fell flattened from the rocky hillside.

Genevra turned quickly. "My preserver!" she shrieked, and fell into the arms of Natty Bumpo, the celebrated Pike Ranger of Donner Lake. (V, 44–45)

Not only do these mock romances now seem banal, but Harte failed to assume in them a consistent critical attitude or tone. While he scorned the fiction of Cooper and Arthur, he admired the stories of Dickens and Dumas, yet the work of all four novelists is travestied. To be sure, "Muck-a-Muck" is more successful than "The Haunted Man," his burlesque of Dickens's *A Christmas Carol,* if only because in the former the parody serves an intrinsic purpose of challenging rather than valorizing a canonical text.

Harte collected most of his early condensed novels in a volume issued by the New York firm of G. W. Carleton Co. in 1867, but he soon regretted the haste with which he entered this contract. He was eager to test the national market for his work, and these stories had been "widely copied and seem[ed] to be popular in the East." The success of the volume, he recognized, would "depend entirely upon its sale in the East" (*L,* 4). Mark Twain worried privately that "Bret . . . is publishing with a Son of a Bitch who will swindle him" (*MTL* II, 30), and the prediction proved appallingly accurate. Harte earned less than $200 from the sale of the first edition. When the book appeared, moreover, he was "incensed" and "mortified" by Frank Bellew's comic illustrations or, as he stated, the "circus clown's dress and the painted grins that Mr. Carleton had scattered through its papers."[30] The edition was critically well-received, however: the *Alta California* praised the "clever imitations" and the *San Francisco Bulletin* elevated Harte to "the foremost rank of American writers" as "a humorist of a high order" and "a master of satire."[31] Even the *Atlantic Monthly* took notice of the "charming parodies, so well known in California."[32] Harte soon thanked Fields for the "generous good will" expressed in the brief review of a book that had been "malformed in its birth. There was an extra kindness in your taking the deformed brat by the hand, and trying to recognize some traces of a parent so far away."[33] Harte retrieved the copyright from Carleton in 1871 by convincing the publisher "that there is neither money nor reputation for him in the reproduction of that monstrosity."[34] After Harte came to terms with Fields, Osgood & Co., the firm issued a new edition of *Condensed Novels* without the offensive illustrations to capitalize on his more recent successes. They were hailed as "the best prose parodies in the language" as late as 1882,[35] and Harte wrote a second series, burlesquing such British authors as Anthony Hope, Conan Doyle, and Rudyard Kipling, during the last months of his life.

Six weeks after the original collection of *Condensed Novels* appeared in New York, Harte's next book, *The Lost Galleon and Other Tales,* appeared from the press of the San Francisco firm Towne and Bacon. It anthologized some 30 of his poems, including the best of his Civil War verse and several of his ballads and satires. Like *Outcroppings,* it was a popular if not a critical success, with approximately 500 copies sold

within three weeks of its publication.[36] The title poem, which Harte
had written for commencement exercises at the College of California
in June 1867,[37] recounts the fanciful legend of a Spanish ship that
cruises the Pacific in search of a day it lost in crossing the international
date line.

> By a computation that still holds good,
> Made by the Holy Brotherhood,
> The San Gregorio will cross that line
> In nineteen hundred and thirty-nine;
> Just three hundred years to a day
> From the time she lost the ninth of May.
> And the folk in Acapulco town,
> Over the waters looking down,
> Will see in the glow of the setting sun
> The sails of the missing galleon. (VIII, 110–11)

In "Padre Junipero's Miracle," another ballad about Spanish colonialism in the New World, the saintly Junipero Serra restores the vitality
of a drought-stricken land by spilling the sacramental wine from his
chalice on the ground:

> From the dry and feverish soil leaped out
> A living fountain; a well-spring burst
> Over the dusty and broad champaign,
> Over the sandy and sterile plain,
> Till the granite ribs and the milk-white stones
> That lay in the valley—the scattered bones—
> Moved in the river and lived again! (VIII, 69)

The poem is a crude, hobbyhorse precursor of "The Waste Land," with
the mission father in the role of the fisher king.

The best of the parodies in the volume, "To the Pliocene Skull,"
lampoons the ostensible discovery of a prehistoric fossil at the bottom
of a well in Calaveras county. On the basis of its position in the soil
strata, Professor J. D. Whitney of the state geological survey had dated
it "to a period anterior to the lava deposits"—that is, before mastodons
and pachyderms roamed the region. This "earliest pioneer," as Harte
elsewhere mused, "must have passed a remarkably active existence in
dodging the scoria and volcanic stones" and fighting with reptiles "for
the limited refection of mussels and shell-fish" (*BHC,* 63). In the

poem, which Harte readily admitted he modeled on Oliver Wendell Holmes's "De Sauty" (Booth 1948, 319), a geologist addresses the skull:

> "Speak, thou awful vestige of the earth's creation,
> Solitary fragment of remains organic!
> Tell the wondrous secret of thy past existence,—
> Speak! thou oldest primate!"

So profound and solemn a command elicits a reply characteristic of Harte's brand of Western Humor:

> "Which my name is Bowers, and my crust was busted
> Falling down a shaft in Calaveras County;
> But I'd take it kindly if you'd send the pieces
> Home to old Missouri!" (VIII, 281)

"To the Pliocene Skull" was widely copied in Eastern papers—Samuel Bowles reprinted its "quaint" stanzas in the *Springfield Republican,* for example.[38] Harte again referred to the controversy in "The Society Upon the Stanislaus" (1869), in which backwoods anthropologists

>   did engage
> In a warfare with the remnants of a palaeozoic age;
> And the way they heaved those fossils in the anger was a sin,
> Till the skull of an old mammoth caved the head of Thompson in.
> (VIII, 133)

On his part, Whitney was undeterred. He argued for the authenticity of the relic in a lecture in New York as late as 1878.[39]

After his partner Webb panned *Outcroppings* in three papers during the winter of 1865–66, Harte was eager to sever his affiliation with the *Californian.* He sent Webb a curt note in October 1866—it is their only extant correspondence—to report that he had successfully brokered the sale of the paper they had launched. The final, ambiguous line of this note oozes sarcasm: "I, in regard to the paper, its present proprietors, & the judiciousness of your bargain say nothing, simply subscribing myself with high regard and considerable satisfaction no longer / Your attorney in fact, / Fr[ancis] Bret Harte."[40] Meanwhile, Warren Sawyer, the managing editor of the *Christian Register,* invited him to write for the Boston Unitarian weekly, and Harte accepted with alacrity on the condition that he be paid $10 in gold per contribution, the same payment he usually received for his articles in California magazines.[41] Mark Twain reported to his family in January 1866 that Harte had "quit the 'Californian'" to "write for a Boston paper hereafter" (*MTL* I, 328). He also agreed to become the regular California correspondent for the *Springfield Republican* several months after meeting its editor Samuel Bowles during the latter's tour of the West in 1865, and over the next few months his reports would appear in the same paper as occasional poems by Bowles's Amherst friend Emily Dickinson. The *Springfield Republican,* more than any other publication, brought Harte to the attention of Easterners in 1866–67. In January 1867, for example, Bowles compared Harte favorably to his western rivals Webb and Twain. Harte, he insisted, "is less demonstrative in his qualities than the others; his humor is more subjective, and his scholarship more thorough and conservative; but we have few newspaper and magazine writers in the East that have so charming and cultivated a fancy, so delicate and innocent a satire."[42] Bowles reiterated the point in May 1867: Harte is "the best of the California humorists after all."[43]

He published 38 essays in these two Massachusetts papers—19 in each—between January 1866 and November 1867. Though he had lived in California for 12 years, he assumed for literary purposes the pose of the expatriate or foreign correspondent. "When you meet" at "the Eastern borders of the continent," he adjured readers in August 1866, think "tenderly" of the "unrelieved sentinels at the Western gate" (*BHC,* 73). Like a missionary, he described California's exotic customs and habits. Californians are gamblers by nature, he reported, famous for fast living and prodigal giving. Like the Arabian Prince, they "prefer their cream tarts with pepper" (*BHC,* 140). Harte repeatedly insisted in these articles that "Californians are naturally cosmopolitan" and "innately liberal," but he admitted that Frederick Law Olmstead's plan for a public common in San Francisco along the lines of Central Park in New York was "too liberal, too large, too comprehensive for this material—and, in such matters, narrow-minded municipality" (*BHC,* 52, 55, 64). He also indicted the subtle restraints on "intellectual life and activity" in the West, even asserting in May 1867 that "the climate is fatal to abstract speculation" (*BHC,* 125). California literature will never come of age, he predicted, as long as the state has "more writers than readers" and "more contributors than subscribers" (*BHC,* 140). He was, it seems, already straining to escape the region.

While these essays are not finished coin, they display an abundance of "color." Like cartloads of raw ore ready for the mill, they contain nuggets of topical comment and local history Harte would later use to "salt" his fiction. He reported to the *Springfield Republican* in June 1866 that he had attended a performance of *Cardinal Richelieu* at Maguire's Opera House with Edwin Forrest in the title role (*BHC, 46*), for example, and a character in his story "A Phyllis of the Sierras" claims to have seen Forrest in the same part "in the theayter" (XXI, 390). Harte's derisive comments on an evangelical revival in San Francisco in an October 1866 letter to the *Christian Register* presage his depiction of a camp meeting in "An Apostle of the Tules" (1885) and his satire of an Elmer Gantry type in "Mr. MacGlowrie's Widow" (1902). A celebrated breach of promise suit Harte discussed in the *Springfield Republican* in April 1867 would later inspire his story "Colonel Starbottle for the Plaintiff" (1902). A liberal on social issues, Harte also used these articles as a forum to protest racial and ethnic intolerance. Despite his tendency to echo racial clichés—e.g., the Chinese are generally "civil and decorous" (*BHC, 115*), inscrutable in expression, and pagan in religion—he was genuinely sympathetic to the plight of the local Chinese and Afro-Americans. Harte deplored the "late riots and outrages on the Chinese" in February 1867 (*BHC, 113*) and attributed it, not without cause, to class rivalries. He would subsequently portray these racial incidents in "Wan Lee, the Pagan" (XVI, 102, 104), his most explicit condemnation of anti–Chinese sentiment. Harte denounced other forms of racial bigotry as well. When blacks were prevented from marching in the Fourth of July parade in 1866 to "spare the sensitive prejudices of our Irish and southern fellow-citizens," he reported, they bore their "humiliation with dignity and silence" (*BHC, 55*).

His ambivalence to things Western extended even to his treatment of the fabled California landscape. Scarcely an essay appeared in either the *Christian Register* or the *Springfield Republican* without Harte commenting on the state's geography or climate, as if these were the subjects he believed Easterners would find most fascinating. He tended to subvert, moreover, the mythology of a paradisiacal California. He confessed in March 1866 that he had "tried for twelve years to appreciate this remarkable climate," albeit to no avail (*BHC, 26*). He bewailed "a country where there is so much clear weather and so few pleasant days" (*BHC, 91*). To be sure, he depicted Berkeley as a bucolic Eden, a veritable Utopia "where the wind doesn't blow and the fogs come not," a "Xanadu of the San Francisco poetical dream" (*BHC, 72*). Elsewhere, however, he warned darkly that the coast is but an "imaginary Utopia" after all, with incidence of poverty, insanity, and suicide well above the norm in the East (*BHC*, 57).

Whereas Harte's initial essays to the papers mainly extol California, his later articles betray an increasing dissatisfaction with the state. "The near fact is that we live in a country unpleasantly new and uncomfortably inchoate," he griped in October 1867 (*BHC*, 145). Bowles, no less a booster of the New West than Horace Greeley, soon dropped Harte's column. Even after he wrote the last of his letters to the *Springfield Republican*, however, Harte enjoyed a virtual immunity from criticism in its pages. Between August 1868 and March 1871, in fact, the paper reprinted the best of his fiction and verse and favorably reviewed his collections of stories and poems. To be sure, the editors in Springfield sometimes fretted that Harte might prove to be a proverbial flash in the pan: "It is still an open question whether he will hold out as he has begun."[44] In the end, regrettably, the answer to this question was an emphatic no. But for the next two or three years, he was at the top of his form.

Chapter Two
Quintessential Harte

After Harte left the *Californian* in mid–1866, he did not write regularly for any California magazine for almost two years. In his early 30s, with Frémont back east and King dead, with the pages of the *Atlantic Monthly* closed to him and his *Condensed Novels* an embarrassment, his literary ambitions seemed futile indeed. He no longer expected to "become the 'future great poet' you kindly prophesy," he wrote an acquaintance in February 1868, only to "satisfy [my]self and a few good fellows" who were his friends.[1] He published a few items over the months in the disreputable *San Francisco News Letter,* a satirical weekly edited by Ambrose Bierce, as well as in other local newspapers, although many of these pieces were unsigned.

The most interesting of these miscellaneous works, "The Right Eye of the Commander," appeared in the *San Francisco Bulletin* on New Year's Eve 1867 and vaguely recalls Hawthorne's "The Minister's Black Veil." The comandante of a Spanish garrison, who has lost an eye to an Indian arrow, is duped by a Yankee bead peddler who fills the orbit with a glass eye. Wherever this "cold, hard, relentless, and unflinching" eye fell, "a shadow fell with it." The commander's "most trusty retainers stammered, blushed, and faltered before him," and children "seemed to be conscious of some hidden sin" (VII, 192–93). In fact, this humorous legend betrays a rather benign view of Spanish and American colonialism. It is set during "that glorious Indian summer of California history," as Harte explains, "around which so much poetical haze still lingers,—that bland, indolent autumn of Spanish rule, so soon to be followed by the wintry storms of Mexican independence and the reviving spring of American conquest" (VII, 185). Much as the commander has lost his eye displacing the ostensibly savage Indians, his reign will yield in turn to the westward expansion of the Anglo-Saxons, represented in the story by the Yankee peddler, thereby subtly allegorizing a conventional theory of social progress through colonialism and conquest.

"The Luck of Roaring Camp"

When Anton Roman decided early in 1868 to launch a monthly magazine similar to the *Atlantic Monthly,* Harte was the obvious choice for editor. For a modest salary, about $100 per issue, he would select the contents, write book reviews, manage a department entitled "Etc.," and contribute a story or poem to the pages of the *Overland Monthly.* He was soon the patron of a stable of young contributors, among them Bierce, Twain, Charles Warren Stoddard, Ina Coolbrith, Joaquin Miller, and Henry George. "I am trying to build up a literary taste on the Pacific slope," he wrote to Henry Bellows in New York. He was by no means sanguine of success. "Perhaps the Bear may get the better of the Locomotive"—Harte here alludes to the magazine's logo—but "I want to make it a good fight while it lasts."[2] If Harte is remembered at all today, he is known for the handful of his own tales published in the *Overland Monthly* between mid–1868 and the end of 1870.

The first issue of the magazine attracted virtually no attention outside California when it appeared in July 1868. Even Harte "failed to discover [in it] anything of that wild and picturesque life which had impressed him, first as a truant schoolboy, and afterwards as a youthful schoolmaster among the mining population" and he determined "to make good the deficiency himself." The next issue contained his story "The Luck of Roaring Camp," a tale on a "distinctively Californian" subject which he considered "a new departure" in western fiction ("Rise," 7). In it, Harte abandoned his earlier, genteel tone of polite condescension to the miners, compressing in the narrative the vernacular voice and inflated style of western humor. According to Ernest R. May, "In no other journal of the time would [the story] have fitted so well. It was this keen consciousness of the demands of his journal that made the monthly under Harte an outstanding magazine."[3]

"The Luck of Roaring Camp" is usually considered a modern parable of the Nativity with the Christ child renamed "the Luck" and the dissolute mining camp a "city of refuge" (VII, 3) gradually redeemed through his influence. Cherokee Sal, the only woman in the camp, dies in childbirth and is buried in a "rude sepulture" (VII, 8). Her son by an unknown father is "swathed" in red flannel and adopted by the men—Kentuck, Stumpy, Jack Hamlin, and others of their ilk—many of them criminals and all of them "reckless" (VII, 5, 3). They decide against hiring a nurse on the grounds no decent woman could be persuaded to settle in Roaring Camp and "they didn't want any more of the other kind"—their "first spasm of propriety" (VII, 9). Instead, Stumpy volunteers ass milk for the boy, whom they christen Thomas (after the brother of Jesus?). "And so the work of regeneration began in Roaring Camp," Harte writes. "Almost imperceptively a change came over the settlement" (VII, 12). The "roughs" begin to observe "stricter habits of personal cleanliness," they no longer curse or swear, and they decorate their cabins with flowers and shrubs (VII, 12–14). Their rehabilitation coincides with "flush times" in the valley: "The claims had yielded enormously" (VII, 16). The expressman, the only outsider admitted to the camp, reports the miners there have "vines and flowers round their houses," "wash themselves twice a day," and "worship an Ingin baby" (VII, 16). The story concludes on a pathetic note: the child is drowned in a spring flash flood while in the embrace of one of the men.

Although tame by modern standards, the story nearly died in galleys. The proofreader and printer objected to the "immoral and indecent" portrayal of Cherokee Sal and to the vulgarities of the miners, as Harte later recalled, and even the publisher feared the story "might imperil the prospects of the magazine" (Dam, 45). Roman subsequently claimed that he had "ordered the article inserted" into the *Overland Monthly*,[4] but Harte recorded a different version of these events: the tale was published only after he threatened to resign as editor if it did not run exactly as written. "I read the story again," he explained, "thought the matter over, and told Mr. Roman that if 'The Luck of Roaring Camp' was not a good and suitable story I was not a good and suitable editor for his magazine. I said that the chief value of an editor lay in the correctness of his judgment, and if his view was the true one, my judgment was clearly at fault" (Dam, 45). The threat worked, and the story appeared to lukewarm if not cool notices in San Francisco. When it "was not denounced as 'improper' and 'corrupting,' it was coldly received as being 'singular' and 'strange'" and a local religious paper complained it would discourage immigration and the "investment of foreign capital" in the state, Harte remembered ("Rise," 7). Fortunately, the unsigned story was universally praised in the East. "The hand that wrote it," the *Springfield Republican* averred, "ought to be able to make a book, or at any rate, to 'contribute to every number'" of the new magazine. Three days later, on 12 September 1868, the editors of the *Springfield Republican* reprinted the tale in its entirety, and by the end of the month they had announced that

none other than "our old friend Harte" had penned "the best magazine
story of the year."[5] Mark Twain thought it "Bret's very best sketch"
(Booth 1954, 493); George Meredith applauded the "shaggy realism"
of the tale and expressed "envy of the writer's power";[6] and James
Fields wrote him to solicit a story similar to "The Luck" for the *Atlantic
Monthly* (Dam, 46). Harte thanked Fields for the offer but explained
that "as Editor of the *Overland Monthly* my duties claim most of my
spare time outside of the Govt. office in wh[ich] I am employed." He
could not resist a jab at the editor who had snubbed his work years
before: "I'll try to find time to send you something." Should the *Overland Monthly,* "still an experiment," fail, "why I dare say I may be able
to do more."[7]

Rather than a sentimental and updated account of the Nativity, ironically, "The Luck of Roaring Camp" seems in retrospect a virtual parody of the gospels. The proofreader and printer for the *Overland Monthly*
objected only to the most obvious elements of the religious satire.
Harte wrote the story not in the guise of a moralist but as a humorist.
He cautions the reader in the opening paragraphs to beware of appearances: the "greatest scamp" among the miners "had a Raphael face,"
for example (VII, 3). As an "irreclaimable" prostitute and "very sinful
woman" (VII, 1), Cherokee Sal is an ironic Madonna who, at her death,
"climbed, *as it were,* that rugged road that led to the stars" (VII, 4,
italics mine). The inserted phrase certainly qualifies the suggestion of
sainthood. Indeed, as Harte writes, "Perhaps the less said of her the
better" (VII, 1). Little Tommy Luck's father is not known, but not
because he is born of a virgin. Similarly, the miners are ironic Magi
whose gifts to the child include stolen silverware, a tobacco box, and
a revolver. Except for a Bible, as Fred Schroeder notes, "all the dona-
tions represent violence, objects of sensual pleasure, or mere monetary
booty."[8] The "roughs" christen the child Thomas Luck in a "ludicrous"
ceremony (VII, 11). His first name recalls the Doubting Apostle, not
Jesus' brother, and his surname, as J. R. Boggan observes, "is not that
of the supposed far-seeing Christ but, rather just the opposite, that of
blind Chance."[9] To be sure, the town launches a program of civic improvement. But what is the net effect of this "spasm of propriety"? The
saloon is refurbished with a new carpet and mirrors and the men begin
to bathe. The narrator admits that, unfortunately, tales "of the [the
child's] sagacity"—in particular, his ability to talk with animals—rest
"upon the statements of prejudiced friends" (VII, 15). They are as spu-
rious and unreliable as similar stories about the Christ child recorded

in the apocryphal Gospel of Thomas. In the final pages, moreover, Roaring Camp simply washes away in a flood of biblical proportions— its "regeneration" comes to naught—and the child is killed, a victim of natural catastrophe. In the last sentence of the story, Kentuck clings to his "frail" body and "drift[s] away into the shadowy river that flows forever to the unknown sea" (VII, 18). These adjectives scarcely commend the child's martyrdom or vicarious sacrifice; on the contrary, they suggest that his death is a random event in a world without design or purpose. What Harte's title neglects to report is that the luck of Roaring Camp is, in the end, all bad.

Seven Stories

The popularity of "The Luck" in the East ensured the success of the *Overland Monthly* under Harte's management and allowed him to follow it "with other stories of a like character" ("Rise," 7). He was no literary realist in these tales, save in the very broadest sense of the term. "His observation of Gold Rush country, character, and society was neither very accurate nor very penetrating," as Wallace Stegner notes.[10] To be sure, he repeatedly claimed that he was "personally cognizant" of all "natural phenomena made use of" in his fiction and that all of his characters "were drawn from life to a greater or less extent" (Dam, 48). Such figures as John Oakhurst, Brown of Calaveras, and Tennessee and his partner are all modeled upon identifiable men. But as "a humble writer of romance" (VII, iv), Harte depicted the West through a filtered lens and in soft light and his characters—whether dandy gamblers, rough miners, genteel schoolmarms, inscrutable Orientals, or gruff stagedrivers—rarely transcend the stereotypical. Like mechanical parts or actors in a stock company, Jack Hamlin and Colonel Culpepper Starbottle each appear in at least 20 melodramas, often in cameo roles. As in *The Old Curiosity Shop* or *Bleak House,* these stories often lapse into pathos.[11] Indeed, according to Twain, Harte once bragged that he was " the best imitator of Dickens in America" (*MTE,* 266), although he shunned Dickens's overt didacticism. He replied to the charge that he excused if not approved acts of overt criminality by protesting he "never moralized or commented upon the action of his heroes" nor "voiced a creed or obtrusively demonstrated an ethical opinion."[12] As he would only belatedly recognize, his best work tapped a tradition of western humor and was written in the style of oral narrative. He was "less interested in dialogue than most local colorists," Harold Kolb observes, "saving his best lines for the narrator."[13] Harte would describe his brand of humorous tale in his late essay "The Rise of the 'Short Story'" (1899), a piece that is part memoir and part literary manifesto. The successful western-humor story, he explained,

> was concise and condensed, yet suggestive. It was delightfully extravagant, or a miracle of under-statement. It voiced not only the dialect, but the habits of thought of a people of locality. It gave a new interest to slang. . . . It was a foe to prolixity of any kind; it admitted no fine writing nor affectation of style. It went directly to the point. It was burdened by no conscientiousness; it was often irreverent; it was devoid of all moral responsibility, but it was often original! By degrees it developed character with its incident, often, in a few lines, gave a striking photograph of a community or a section, but always reached its conclusion without an unnecessary word. ("Rise," 3)

Little wonder Harte's California stories all bear a close family resemblance.

As in "The Luck," the menagerie of character types in "The Outcasts of Poker Flat" are victims of blind chance and freak disaster. First published in the *Overland Monthly* for January 1869, this story is set in 1850, scarcely two years after the discovery of gold at Sutter's Mill, although the settlement has already begun to assume civilized or "Sabbath" airs. The local economy is based not on mining, as in Roaring Camp, but on gambling. Harte had first mentioned the "arcadian hamlet" of Poker Flat in a February 1867 letter to the *Springfield Republican.* There he explained that "most of the portable property" in town changed hands several times each winter "through the agency of seven-up or bluff," which the "gentle villagers" play to "amuse themselves" (*BHC,* 112). The chief of the outcasts, John Oakhurst, is run out of the village not because he is a gambler, but because he is so successful a gambler. As its name suggests, the town is built on a plain or *flat,* but the term may be understood in an ironic sense, too: *flat* also connotes *broke* or *busted.* The very name of the town thus anticipates the plot. Each of the outcasts has been expelled in "a spasm of virtuous reaction, quite as lawless and ungovernable as any of the acts that had provoked it," by the local vigilance committee (VII, 19–20). Obviously, this "spasm" is akin to that "spasm of propriety" that led to the ironic reformation of Roaring Camp. The outcasts—Oakhurst, a whore called "the Duchess," her madam Mother Shipton, and a thief and drunkard known as Uncle Billy—head for the neighboring town of Sandy Bar, a name that sounds like the place where, according to the parable of Jesus in the gospel of Matthew, the foolish man built his house. In any event, Sandy Bar has not "yet experienced the regenerating influences of Poker Flat" (VII, 22). The action of the tale is set entirely in the "steep mountain range" between these two towns, quite literally on the cusp between civilization and the wilderness (VII, 22). The outcasts meet up with the children of Nature, Tom Simson "the Innocent" and his young wife Piney Woods, in the forest; that is, the sinners and the sinless become virtually indistinguishable in a state of nature. Like a serpent in the garden, the rascal Uncle Billy rustles the mules and abandons the group, but the remaining outcasts are reformed by events. The Duchess blushes at Piney's innocent remark that she must be "used to fine things"; Oakhurst "doesn't say 'cards' once"; all three of them join the Innocent and Piney in "a rude camp-meeting hymn" to while away the time when a sudden snowstorm blows up (VII, 29, 30). As Harte describes the scene, "The pines rocked, the storm eddied and whirled above the miserable group, and the flames of their altar leaped heavenward" (VII, 30). Barred by law and the blizzard from returning to Poker Flat, Oakhurst and the ladies of easy virtue become models of moral behavior: Mother (read, Mother Superior) Shipton gives her ration of food to Piney and starves to death; Oakhurst piles enough wood beside their cabin to "last a few days longer" and coolly plays out his losing hand "with the usual percentage in favor of the dealer" before "handing in his checks" and committing suicide; and the Duchess rests her head upon Piney's shoulder, "the younger and purer pillowing the head of her soiled sister upon her virgin breast" (VII, 34, 21, 36, 35). When their frozen bodies are discovered a few days later, Harte adds, "you could scarcely have told from the equal peace that dwelt upon them which was she that had sinned" (VII, 35). The outcasts are regenerated in a state of nature, yet, like Kentuck and Tommy Luck, they die as the result of a natural disaster. Their reformation, like Roaring Camp's, is finally meaningless, and the conclusions to both stories are contrived and pathetic. "The Outcasts" is a lesser tale only because it lacks the ironic or satirical texture of "The Luck." Still, Ina Coolbrith thought the story "splendid" when it first appeared;[14] Twain ranked it "next to 'The Luck' unquestionably" (Booth 1954, 493); Howells considered it the "more representative" of Harte's "most characteristic" work;[15] Frank Norris parodied it mercilessly in his perverted tale "The Hero of Tomato Can"; and Arthur Hobson Quinn would hail it as late as 1936 as "a masterpiece" (Quinn, 235).

"Miggles," a Dickensian sketch about a reformed prostitute with the proverbial heart of gold, appeared originally in the June 1869 *Overland Monthly*. The narrator meets the unlikely heroine when Yuba Bill's stagecoach, on which he is a passenger, is diverted to her cabin during a storm. She had kept a saloon and dance hall in Marysville where, as she declares, "everybody had the right to know me" and she was "popular with everybody" (VII, 50, 51). She had sold her business six years earlier, however, and moved to the outback to nurse her friend Jim, a syphilitic invalid. Jim "used to know me," she explains, "and spent a heap of money upon me" before he fell ill as a result of his "mighty free and wild like . . . way of life" (VII, 50). Although advised he "would never get better" and "would be a baby all his life," Miggles refuses to abandon him: "perhaps," she says, "it was that I never had a baby" (VII, 51). The narrator implicitly compares her to Mary Magdalene "in the sweet old story" when, the next morning, she "bathed the feet of him she loved" (VII, 54). Harte would include a brief sequel to this popular story in "A Night on the Divide" 25 years later: the "charming and historic" Miggles eventually "decided to accompany her paralytic lover to the San Francisco hospital" (XIV, 266). As Howells remarked, in her time "good criminals abounded, and ladies with pasts were of a present behavior so self-devoted that they could often put their unerring sisters to the blush."[16]

The story of Miggles is also virtually unique among Harte's stories for its satire of traditional sex roles. His racial and religious toleration notwithstanding, Harte had criticized feminism in the person of a Bloomer who paraded on the streets of San Francisco in an August 1866 letter to the *Springfield Republican*. Admittedly, such "progressive" attitudes were the "product of an older civilization" but, he protested, California society "is too material in tone already; we cannot afford to accept any innovation which tends to lower the standard of female modesty—to make [women] more masculine and confident" (*BHC*, 74). However, in "Miggles," a tale of ironic role reversal, Harte imagines a female type who is economically independent and protects a helpless male (VII, 52). They live together in an unconventional relationship sanctioned not by law but by mutual affection. As Miggles notes, "if we were man and wife, now, we'd both know that I was *bound* to do what I do now of my own accord" (VII, 53). Something of a mountain woman, she keeps a half-grown grizzly bear for a watchdog. She wears a dress, to be sure, but one of "coarse blue stuff," presumably denim (VII, 43). She punctuates her conversation with "expletives, the use of which had generally been yielded to [her] sex" (VII, 46–47), the narrator reports. Indeed, "her very frankness suggested a perfect sexual equality that was cruelly humiliating to the younger members of our party" (VII, 48). Although the narrator insists that males represent "the stronger portion of humanity," the men in the story unwittingly behave like stereotypical women when in private they crowd together, "whispering, snickering, smiling, and exchanging suspicions" about their host and her companion (VII, 48–49). In the end, Miggles is a much more sympathetic figure than any of the prurient men who gossip about her.

"Tennessee's Partner," first printed in the *Overland Monthly* for October 1869, represents the high-water mark of Harte's achievement in fiction. On the surface, it seems a perfectly straightforward tale of loyalty and friendship. After the petty criminal Tennessee elopes with his Partner's bride, the Partner apparently "took the loss of his wife simply and seriously, as was his fashion." The two men are immediately reconciled when Tennessee returns to Sandy Bar alone, to the dismay of the "boys who had gathered in the cañon to see the shooting" (VII, 58). Later, the Partner appears to defend Tennessee at his trial for highway robbery: "He lays for a stranger, and he fetches that stranger. And you lays for *him,* and you fetches *him*; and the honors is easy" (VII, 63). The Partner even tries, to no avail, to bribe the judge and jury with $1,700 in gold if they will simply release the defendant. After Tennessee is hung as per the sentence of Judge Lynch, his Partner claims the body and gives it a decent burial, only then to pine away and die. With his last breath he greets Tennessee in the Great Beyond. Even so brief a synopsis of the plot frames its major critical flaw, according to Cleanth Brooks and Robert Penn Warren: "The difficulty with this story has to do with the credibility of the actions of Tennessee's partner. . . . Bret Harte is so thoroughly obsessed with the pathos of the partner's loyalty that he has devoted no thought to the precise nature of the basis of that loyalty."[17] Read in this way, the story evades the psychological issues raised by Tennessee's wife-stealing. Why, as Twain wondered, does he make "his hero *welcome back* a man who has committed against him that sin which neither the great nor the little ever forgive?" (Booth 1954, 494).

Linda Burton answers this question, albeit not very convincingly, by contending that the two men are homosexual companions. As with a married couple, the spouse has assumed his partner's name. Tennessee and his Partner are by turns involved with the same woman because, according to Burton, they "were seeking their heterosexuality and, at the same time, attempting to deny their homosexuality by having a close relationship with a woman, something neither man obviously found successful."[18] Even during his brief marriage, the Partner continues to live with Tennessee; when Tennessee steals his wife, the Partner takes the loss "simply and seriously" because the marriage was doomed from the start. Burton notes that the Partner greets Tennessee "with affection" when he returns to Sandy Bar, whereupon they resume an "intimacy" the other miners suspect is rooted in a "copartnership in crime" (VII, 58). The Partner attempts to bribe the judge and jury to save his mate, or so the argument goes, and he arranges the "obsequies" with such care because he is burying his lover.

Unfortunately, both the New Critical and homoerotic analyses of "Tennessee's Partner" ignore its subtle irony. Harte has, in effect, set a trap for the unwary. "You could never be sure of Harte," as Howells recalled; "he could only by chance be caught in earnest about anything or anybody" (*LFA,* 296). The narrator betrays as little expression in relating this story as the poker-faced Partner reveals in plotting revenge on the man who stole his wife. "Harte tricks his readers all the while he seems to be trying to satisfy their pious presuppositions," William F. Connor contends, just as the Partner "successfully bamboozles the mining camp folk."[19] That is, Harte deftly structures the story around the Partner's elaborate scheme to avenge his loss of a wife, the act of victimization, which is central to western humor. (Recall the series of such acts that occur in Twain's "Jumping Frog" sketch.) Obviously, the miners in Sandy Bar expect the Partner to exact revenge. Their "indignation" at his failure to shoot Tennessee on sight "might have found vent in sarcasm," as the narrator adds, " but for a certain look in Tennessee's Partner's eye that indicated a lack of humorous appreciation" (VII, 58). The Partner has already hatched his plot, and he now bides his time. He exploits the opportunity to serve frontier justice when he appears in court at precisely the moment Tennessee's prosecution has become "irksomely thoughtful" (VII, 61). The trial becomes at this point something of a poker game, with Tennessee folding his cards—"I don't take any hand in this yer game" (VII, 61)—and the Partner in the role of the dealer. "I play this yer hand alone" and "This yer is a lone hand, played alone, and without my pardner," as he says (VII, 63, 64). He summarizes Tennessee's crime as well as could any prosecuting attorney and then bluffs the judge and jury by apparently offering them a bribe. The court, no longer bored, is suddenly galvanized, for the "unparalleled insult" erases "any wavering determination of Tennessee's fate" (VII, 65). On his part, "Tennessee laughed" (VII, 64). He understands the rules of the game played out in the courtroom. "Euchred, old man!" he says to the Partner, then shakes his hand. The gesture is neither one of gratitude for the failed attempt to save his life nor one of friendly parting, but a way of congratulating the Partner for winning the pot.

The final paragraphs of the story, however bathetic they may seem, are no less liable to misinterpretation. After Tennessee is lynched—or "when the weak and foolish deed was done" (VII, 65–66)—the Partner unceremoniously hauls the corpse in a donkey cart usually used "in carrying dirt" to a shallow grave at an "unpicturesque" site near his cabin (VII, 66, 68). He inters the body, significantly enough, in the very garden he had cultivated during "the brief days of [his] matrimonial felicity" with the woman Tennessee stole from him (VII, 68). In his eulogy to the assembled townsfolk, the Partner emphasizes his own long-suffering fidelity to the friendship Tennessee betrayed: "It ain't the first time that I've packed him on my back, as you see'd me now. It ain't the first time that I brought him to this yer cabin when he couldn't help himself; it ain't the first time that I and Jinny have waited for him on yon hill, and picked him up and so fetched him home, when he couldn't speak and didn't know me" (VII, 69).

Under the circumstances, he asks implicitly, who can blame him for wanting this man dead? After the funeral (or "fun'l," as the Partner calls it in a revealing verbal clue), the crowd disperses. Seen from a distance, the Partner sits "upon the grave" with his face apparently "buried in his red bandana handkerchief." But is he weeping? As the narrator explains, "you couldn't tell his face from his handkerchief at that distance, and this point remained undecided" (VII, 70). He is, more likely, sitting on the grave triumphantly. Although Charles May contends that he soon dies of guilt for having incited the lynching,[20] a more reasonable explanation can be found: like Hawthorne's Roger Chillingworth, Tennessee's Partner has made revenge the raison d'être of his life; and just as Chillingworth wastes away in the last chapter of *The Scarlet Letter,* so too does the Partner. If Tennessee and his Partner are reconciled in heaven, as Harte implies in the final lines of the story, it is because, like Chillingworth and Arthur Dimmesdale, they "may, unawares, have found their earthly stock of hatred and antipathy transmuted into golden love" in the afterlife.[21]

In "The Idyl of Red Gulch" (December 1869), Harte literally invented the stock character of the Eastern schoolmarm, here named Miss Mary, the literary forebear of such vestals of the cult of civilization as

Molly Stark Wood in Owen Wister's *The Virginian* and Amy Fowler in Stanley Kramer's *High Noon*. Like others of the type, Miss Mary is a pretty young emigrant who has come west "for the sake of health and independence" (VII, 82) and who acts, often unconsciously, as a civilizing agent upon a settlement but one remove from barbarism. Her influence is nowhere more evident than in the reformation of a local miner and drunkard named Sandy. Despite "some faint signs of dissipation," he is quite "amiable-looking" while sober (VII, 77) and, predictably, they fall in love. Late in the afternoon of the last day of the school term, however, Miss Mary is visited by the "dubious" and "overdressed mother" of one of her pupils (VII, 83, 79)—that is, by another of Harte's gallant whores—who has come to ask a favor: "take my Tommy," she begs the teacher. "Only take him out of this wicked life, this cruel place, this home of shame and sorrow" and put him in "some good school, where you can go and see him, and help him to—to—to forget his mother." When he is older, "tell him his father's name," Alexander Morton, "whom they call here Sandy!" Although shaken by the revelation of her lover's profligacy, Miss Mary agrees to assume custody of the boy and she gives "the happy mother" a message for his father: "Tell him I have taken his child, and tell him—he must never see—see—the child again" (VII, 85–87). She leaves on the stagecoach with Tommy the next day, never to return. Whereas both Molly Wood and Amy Fowler in the end compromise their genteel principles and capitulate to love, Miss Mary abandons Red Gulch to its vice and corruption and flees with the innocent boy to the more refined and civil East.

The mixed-blood Jack Hamlin, who is mentioned incidentally in "The Idyl of Red Gulch," appears to fuller advantage in Harte's next story for the *Overland Monthly*, "Brown of Calaveras" (March 1870). If in the former tale Harte problematizes the settlement of the West by failing to consummate the marriage of the Eastern schoolmarm and Sandy, in the latter story he complicates the problem by having his hero save the failing marriage of an Eastern beauty and her jealous husband by admonishing them to leave the West. Hamlin is a cynic by trade and a gambler by profession, a sort of hard-boiled John Oakhurst with a gun and an "infelix reputation" (VII, 99). A "sentimental blackleg" and "kindred spirit" with the sparrow hawk (VII, 93), he is also something of a tomcat with women. He is struck by the rare beauty of Brown's wife Sue, lately arrived from the East, when they meet aboard the Wingdam stage. Like Sandy Morton, Brown has been sexually profligate and "disfigured by dissipation" (VII, 94–95), though he becomes a pillar of the community after winning enough money at poker through Hamlin's clandestine intercession to buy out his partners in a gold mine. He is eventually elected to the state assembly and a street in Wingdam is named in his honor. Yet "as he waxed wealthy and fortunate" he grew ever more "pale, thin, and anxious" (VII, 98) as a consequence of his floundering marriage to the lovely Sue. He no longer even tries to "interfere with his wife's social liberty," Harte explains, because "his first and only attempt was met by an outburst from Mrs. Brown that terrified him into silence" (VII, 98). "Her room's t'other end of the hall," Brown confides to Hamlin during one of the gambler's infrequent visits to his mansion. "It's more'n six months since we've lived together, or met, except at meals" (VII, 100). Worse yet, "she writes to somebody" and has packed her belongings as though she plans to "steal away like a thief!" (VII, 102). Unbeknown to Brown, ironically, Sue's secret lover is Hamlin, who has come to the mansion at her behest to fetch her away. After Brown confesses his love for her and solicits his friend's advice, Hamlin vindicates the implicit trust. He urges Brown to "sell out all you've got, take your wife with you, and quit the country. It ain't no place for you nor her. Tell her she must go; make her go, if she won't" (VII, 105). Hamlin understands full well that the moral climate of California is inhospitable to such effete Eastern types as the Browns—that, as Harte had written the *Christian Register* in July 1866, it "exacts the greatest labor, endurance, energy and pluck, as the conditions of success" and that while the "prizes offered are often high" the "blanks are many and frequent" (*BHC,* 57). Much as Miss Mary rescues Tommy from the spiritual sinkhole of Red Gulch, the Browns must escape the West to save their marriage, the most elemental of all social bonds. Significantly, Harte had begun to plot his own return east when he wrote these stories (Booth 1948, 320).

In "Mr. Thompson's Prodigal" (July 1870), the slightest of his *Overland Monthly* tales, Harte again associated the West with wickedness and dissipation. California is, in this ironic retelling of Jesus' parable, the "far country" where the prodigal son squanders his birthright in riotous living. The elder Thompson, a rich man who has lately "experienced religion," journeys west to seek and reclaim his lost son (XVII, 122). Although his "quest was the subject of some satire" among the roughs (XVII, 121), it is apparently successful: the old man is mugged one night on the streets of San Francisco by a young thug who resembles his boy and who answers to the name Thompson. "[I]t was known the next morning that Mr. Thompson had found his son" (XVII, 125), Harte reports, though the discovery gave the old man little pleasure. Even after a year "he had little love for the son he had regained," so he decides to host a "feast of reconciliation" in the "fine house he had built on the sandhills" of the city (XVII, 125, 126). A man "shabbily dressed" and "evidently in liquor" interrupts this formal dinner, however, and after greeting the ostensible son he collapses on the floor (XVII, 129, 130). This dissolute fellow, as it happens, is the real Charles Thompson. The man who had taken the name and the accompanying inheritance confesses he is an impostor. "I had no father I could claim," he explains. "I never knew a home but this. I was tempted. I have been happy,—very happy." He kisses the "grizzled head" of the father and disappears forever into the "tumult of a great city" (XVII, 133). Harte thus practically inverts the biblical parable: the real son remains unconverted at the end, and the "elder brother," instead of resenting the prodigal's untimely entrance, proves his love for the father by renouncing all claims to the estate.

In "The Iliad of Sandy Bar" (November 1870), a sort of companion piece to "Tennessee's Partner," Harte dramatized his estrangement from his sometime friend and rival Mark Twain. At Twain's request, Harte had "read all the MS" of *The Innocents Abroad* in the spring of 1868 "& told me what passages, paragraphs & chapters to leave out—& I followed orders strictly. It was a kind thing for Harte to do." When the book appeared the next year, moreover, Harte had reviewed it in the *Overland Monthly,* applauding its 650 "pages of open and declared fun" and placing its author in the "foremost [rank] among Western humorists."[22] Unfortunately, however, Harte did not receive the advance copy of the book he had requested, and so he sent Twain a "*most daintily contemptuous & insulting letter.*" By the time "The Ilaid of Sandy Bar" appeared in the *Overland Monthly,* they had been "off" for "many months" (*AS,* vii–viii). This story describes the bitter and "inexplicable" quarrel of two former partners, Matthew Scott (Harte) and Henry York (Twain), owners of the "Amity Claim," who had earlier earned by their "amiability and grave tact" the title of "The Peacemakers" in a "community not greatly given to the passive virtues" (XVII, 103). Even though their common claim (California local color?) seems "worked out" and "worthless," it becomes the bone of their contention in a court battle. Scott wins the verdict, "which York instantly appealed" (XVII, 107). Each of them harasses the other by occult and other means: flooded land, libelous gossip, vandalism, and so forth. The feud escalates into rival campaigns for the state legislature, a contest Scott also wins when he declares that "thar's one thing [York] didn't charge me with, and, maybe, he's forgotten. For three years, gentlemen, I was that man's pardner!" (XVII, 114). When Scott leaves for Sacramento, "York went abroad"—much as Twain joined the *Quaker City* excursion to Europe and the Holy Land in late 1867—"and for the first time in many years, distance and a new atmosphere isolated the old antagonists" (XVII, 115). Three years later, to be sure, York returns to Sandy Bar, or Riverside as the camp has been renamed, and the story ends with a deathbed reconciliation between the two men much as, in the spring of 1872, Harte and Twain would at least temporarily resume their old intimacy.

"The Heathen Chinee"

While Harte earned his reputation in the East largely for these seven stories in the *Overland Monthly,* he also contributed some 36 unsigned reviews as well as more than 20 poems to its pages. Most of the reviews—of such books as Emerson's *Society and Solitude,* Elizabeth Stuart Phelps's *The Gates Ajar,* Harriet Beecher Stowe's *Oldtown Folks,* and Thomas Wentworth Higginson's *Army Life in a Black Regiment*—are utterly forgettable, although Patrick Morrow concludes they are "honest and surprisingly modern" in their "consistent plea for realistic writing."[71] Of the poems, at least one became a minor classic of satirical verse: "Plain Language from Truthful James," more popularly known as "The Heathen Chinee." As Duckett explains, in the context of Harte's career this poem "can have but one interpretation: it is a satiric attack on race prejudice" (Duckett 1957, 242). As early as April 1863, in a "Bohemian Paper" for the *Golden Era,* Harte opined that the Chinese are "generally honest, faithful, simple, and painstaking" and he attributed "the vulgar clamor about servile and degraded races" in the campaign to restrict Chinese immigration to "the conscious hate and fear with inferiority always regards the possibility of even-handed justice" (VII, 245, 246–47). In a letter to the *Springfield Republican* in February 1867, he observed that the Chinese were "gradually deposing the Irish from their old, recognized positions in the ranks of labor" because as "servants they are quick-witted, patient, obedient and faithful." He predicted that "John Chinaman" would "eventually supplant Bridget and Patrick in menial occupations" (*BHC,* 114).

"Plain Language from Truthful James" ridicules class resentment at precisely this point: the economic threat the Chinese posed to the Anglo underclass in California. For "ways that are dark / And for tricks that are vain," declares the narrator, "The heathen Chinee is peculiar." Invited to play euchre, a game he pretends he "did not understand," the "childlike and bland" Ah Sin is a more subtle cheat than either James or his partner Bill Nye. (The newspaper humorist F. B. Apter took his pseudonym from this latter character.) Nye's sleeve "was stuffed full of aces and bowers, / And the same with intent to deceive," as James allows.

> But the hands that were played
>   By that heathen Chinee,
> And the points that he made,
>   Were quite frightful to see,—
> Till at last he put down a right bower,
>   Which the same Nye had dealt unto me.

Ah Sin beats Nye at his own game and in more ways than one. "We are ruined by Chinese cheap labor," he shouts—the hypocritical slogan of displaced workers and the Democratic establishment in California at the time—and "he went for that heathen Chinee." Not only had Ah Sin concealed 12 jacks in his sleeves, he had polished his fingernails with wax to mark cards in a game "he did not understand" (VIII, 129–131). Like Babo in Melville's "Benito Cereno," Ah Sin confounds the racist assumptions of narrator and reader alike.

Harte never quite understood the popularity of the poem, which he formally modeled upon Swinburne's "Atalanta in Calydon." He wrote it, from all indications, months and perhaps years before he published it, and it appeared as little more than page filler inserted at the last minute in the September 1870 issue of the *Overland Monthly*. He reportedly once claimed it was "the worst poem I ever wrote, possibly the worst poem anyone ever wrote" (Stewart, 181). Nevertheless, it was soon issued in broadside, set to music, and reprinted in newspapers across the country, becoming in time one of the most familiar verses of the century. (Horatio Alger, Jr., for example, quoted it in no fewer than three juvenile novels between 1872 and 1879.)[24] Unfortunately, the poem was often misread as a burlesque of the inscrutable Oriental that exploits, rather than resists, the stereotype. By one account, President Ulysses Grant postponed a message to Congress on the "Chinese problem" after it "made the whole matter the occasion of hilarity" (Stewart, 180). As late as 1951, the poem was presumed to illustrate the "grave danger to which our country and civilization were exposed" by immigration.[25] Whether or not Truthful James spoke plainly, it seems, Harte's language was liable to misinterpretation.

Editorial Matters

Despite the success of the *Overland Monthly,* Harte's relations with its owners were stormy, with occasional gusts and intermittent bluster. Although its circulation rose to some 3,000 copies per month by the end of 1869, publisher Roman sold the magazine to John H. Carmany for $7,500 early in 1870.[26] His impression of Harte years later was rather hostile: "He was a dandy; a dainty man, too much of a woman to rough it in the mines."[27] Harte also sparred with the new owner, who was inclined to interfere with the administration of the magazine, for the rest of his tenure as editor. In fact, he presented Carmany with an ultimatum in June 1870: he would continue with the magazine for another year only if he were given "exclusive control, as formerly, of its literary and critical conduct"; he occupied a private office "as formerly"; and he received a monthly salary of $200, plus "the same amount paid other contributors per page" for his stories and poems (*L,* 7). He added that these terms were not negotiable, "were made after careful deliberation, and are, in my opinion, essential to the safety of the magazine."[28] Although he acceded to Harte's demands, Carmany subsequently charged the editor with "stealing money delivered to him to be paid to contributors," at least according to Mark Twain (*MT–HL,* I, 235–36). Whether this allegation was true, Carmany would later grouse he had "spent $30,000 to make Bret Harte famous."[29]

Under the circumstances, Harte prudently weighed other, more lucrative opportunities. The New York firm Harper & Brothers offered him between $100 and $150 "for every poem" accepted for the *Weekly, Monthly,* or *Bazar.*[30] The publishers of the *Lakeside Monthly* in Chicago approached him about assuming the editorship of their magazine, although he spurned this overture. Parke Godwin tried to recruit him to take over *Putnam's,* and he replied in July 1870 that he "should give myself up to it entirely" for "a salary of at least $5,000 per annum, *guaranteed for one year.*"[31] F. P. Church, editor of *The Galaxy,* also solicited a series of contributions, to which Harte replied with haughty

sarcasm:" . . . if I chose to furnish the amount of 'copy' required by
The Galaxy, I could by disposing of it elsewhere, realize twice the sum
wh[ich] *The Galaxy* offers. During the last 18 mo[nth]s I have [re-
ceived] propositions for more copy than I could possibly furnish . . .
and it is but due to your apparent frank concern for my well-doing to
assure you that *The Galaxy* has made me the lowest and least advan-
tageous offer wh[ich] I have yet had the honor to receive from any
one."[32] He had been asked by the Boston firm of Fields, Osgood as
early as the spring of 1869, in fact, to prepare an edition of his *Overland
Monthly* stories and the best of his earlier California sketches—a volume
that appeared to celebratory notices in April 1870.[33] In late June 1870,
Fields, Osgood offered him $5,000 annually—"the income named by
me as essential to my removing East"—to "connect myself" with the
Atlantic Monthly (Booth 1948, 321). When his partisans in the Bay
Area got wind of this proposition, they tried to entice him to remain
in San Francisco with a patronage job: the regents of the University of
California offered him a position as Professor of Recent Literature and
Curator of the Library and Museum—the same title James Russell
Lowell held at Cornell University—at a monthly salary of $300. As he
explained to the Boston publishers, this job would "not interfere with
my editorial work" on the *Overland Monthly,* and both offices together
would pay him "ab[ou]t $6,000 (gold) per annum. Can you do as well
for me, and how?" (Booth 1948, 321). Fields, Osgood promptly raised
the ante and, in the end, Harte declined the university appointment
on the grounds "it would interfere with his profession" and a visit he
planned to "the Atlantic States."[34] He published a second book, a collection of poems, with Fields, Osgood in time for the holiday trade in
1870, and six editions were sold out in five days after it was announced.[35] Confident he could strike a deal in Boston, he resigned from
the *Overland Monthly* at the close of the year. Carmany, whose investment had suddenly turned sour, desperately tried to convince Harte to
remain as editor by matching the offer—$5,000 annually, plus $100
for each story or poem, plus a quarter interest in the magazine
(Stewart, 184)—but then backed out. "Can I ever be sufficiently grateful to him for expressing so sublimely in himself the quintessence of
California ignorance blindness and self-conceit[?]" Harte later asked
rhetorically (Booth 1948, 324). He had, as he said, "burned his ships"
(Young, 45). The "best-known and best-liked writer in light literature
which we have," Harte left California forever with his family in tow
on 2 February 1871, "to take up his residence permanently in the

East," as the *Alta California* reported on that day.[36] He had already accepted an invitation to attend a meeting of the Boston Saturday Club, the most exclusive literary circle in the country, on 25 February. "I would this had been put off until the tidal wave of my present popularity has subsided, or until I had done something more worthy," he protested to W. D. Howells, "but my daemon wills otherwise and I go three thousand miles to be found out" (Booth 1948, 322). These last facetious words were, as it happened, oddly prophetic.

Chapter Three

From Fifth Avenue to Grub Street

Annus Mirabilis

With his departure for the East, Harte became both literally and figuratively a journeyman writer. En route, he left the manuscript of his poem "The Hawk's Nest" with the editors of the *Chicago Art Review,* and he paused in New York to fulfill his "engagement with the Harpers for a few poems, illustrative of Spanish life in California,"[1] before arriving in the Hub on 24 February. He spent a charmed week in Cambridge among the stars in the New England literary pantheon—Howells, Emerson, Fields, Lowell, Longfellow, Dana, Holmes—and a week later he concluded an agreement with Fields, Osgood to write exclusively for their magazines for a year. The circulation of the *Atlantic Monthly* had plummeted over the previous twelvemonth by as many as 50,000 subscribers as a result of the flap over Harriet Beecher Stowe's defense of Lady Byron in the September 1869 issue.[2] Harte was, it seems, the indirect beneficiary of the controversy, his the marquee name on which the firm hoped to rebuild circulation and recoup advertising revenue. "I have been offered $15,000 per annum and not less than $7,500" and "I have just accepted $10,000 per year from J. R. Osgood," he wrote Ambrose Bierce in early March, "merely for the exclusive right to such of my poems & sketches as I may turn out in that space" (Booth 1948, 324). The contract—the most lucrative to date in the history of American publishing—was finalized on 6 March 1871 and specified that his contributions were not to number fewer than 12 during the year. "I have made some pecuniary sacrifice for the sake of keeping my books in the one house, and of giving a preference to my English publisher," he allowed.[3] He soon moved his clan to Fifth Avenue in New York and began to spend money he had not yet been paid, much less earned, on monogramed stationery, tailored suits, and a summer in Newport. "I shall want some money soon, and regularly, if I make my household life here," he wrote Osgood from New York less than a month after signing the contract.[4] "Just now I want $600, & would be obliged if you would remit your check for that amount by return mail."[5]

He arrived in the East, as Howells opined years later, "after the age of observation was past for him" (*LFA,* 299). (Harte left his eye in San Francisco?) His performance as Phi Beta Kappa poet at Harvard University in June was but an intimation of trouble to come: unable to complete an original piece for the "august" occasion, he merely reworked some lines he first published in the *Golden Era* in 1862 and the result was "a jingle so trivial, so out of keeping, so inadequate that his enemies, if he ever truly had any, must have suffered from it almost as much as his friends" (*LFA,* 300). For whatever reason—the change of geography, the short-term security, the distractions of literary celebrity—Harte became decidedly dilatory in honoring the contract. "He will take his time about his work as all authors must who would do their best and enhance their reputations," the *New York Tribune* editorialized,[6] in effect providing him with a ready excuse for failure. Walt Whitman remarked later that Harte—who had rejected "Passage to India" when it was submitted to the *Overland Monthly*—"cultivated foppishness and superiority" after settling in New York.[7] The first piece he wrote—"Lothaw," a send-up of Disraeli's *Lothair* in his old "condensed novel" style—was relegated to *Every Saturday,* first cousin to the *Atlantic Monthly* in the firm's family of magazines; the second—"Handsome is as Handsome Does," a "condensed" version of Charles Reade's *Put Yourself in His Place*—was rejected altogether because Fields, Osgood held exclusive American rights to Reade's fiction and worried the satire would offend the British writer (*L,* 14).

The first story Harte published in the *Atlantic Monthly* under the terms of the agreement, "The Poet of Sierra Flat," finally appeared in the July 1871 issue to a chorus of yawns. Deliberately or not, Harte subtly ridiculed his western material in this tale; that is, he assumed the patronizing tone of the Brahmins toward his comic frontier types. The "enterprising editor" of the *Sierra Flat Record* agrees to print, for the price of an advertisement, the doggerel of a sissy-poet named Milton Chubbuck, who is vaguely modeled upon the author. Like "The Heathen Chinee," Chubbuck's verse is so hackneyed it becomes "instantly" popular around "camp-fires, in lonely cabins, in flaring barrooms and noisy saloons" (XVII, 159). Chubbuck is hailed from Poker Flat to Roaring Camp as a rising literary genius, and he even receives congratulatory letters from Longfellow, Tennyson, and Browning.

Pressed to declaim "an original poem" at the local dance hall (like Harte at Harvard) he agrees but, after the curtain rises, he "faltered, tottered, and staggered to the wings" (XVII, 165). In the gimmicky and anticlimactic conclusion, the reader learns that Chubbuck is a double imposter—a woman posing as a man posing as a poet. In all, Harte betrays in the story an uneasy sense of his own success, his sudden (and undeserved?) popularity. Even the surname *Chubbuck* seems in retrospect an ironic comment on his own fat contract.

Technically, Harte supplied his publishers with more than the specified minimum of 12 contributions while the agreement was in force. Howells clearly erred in alleging later that he had written only "one story and two or three poems" during the year (*LFA,* 301). However, three of the pieces appeared in *Every Saturday,* and five of the nine items published in the *Atlantic Monthly* were hackneyed poems. That is, Harte complied with the letter of the contract, although he was surely overpaid for the amount and quality of the work he produced. Tom Hood complained that Harte's "A Newport Romance" (October 1871) was "scarcely up to his standard,"[8] for example, and even the author confessed it was rather "poor stuff" (*L,* 15). From all indications, Osgood had lost faith in Harte by late November 1871,[9] although the author tried "to adjust the little differences which exist between us in regard to my performance" under the contract, particularly his "delay in execution," by sending him a poem in April 1874 (Duckett 1964, 85).

In the end, only one of Harte's articles for the *Atlantic Monthly* compares favorably with his work for the *Overland Monthly:* "How Santa Claus Came to Simpson's Bar," a Christmas story in the March (!) 1872 issue. Like the miners in Roaring Camp, the quaint roughs in this tale are humanized through a selfless act of charity. Invited on Christmas Eve 1862 to the cabin of an improvident miner known simply as the Old Man, they meet his pathetic son Johnny, deathly ill with fever, "childblains," "roomatiz," and "biles" (XVII, 63). They take up a collection of coins when they overhear Johnny ask the Old Man "Wot's Chrismiss, anyway? Wot's it all about?" (XVII, 66). Dick Bullen, "the or, rariest" of all the "gang o' lazy drunken loafers" (XVII, 64), rides all night and braves flood, sexual temptation, and a robbery attempt to buy "a few poor toys—cheap and barbaric" but "bright with paint and tinsel"—for the boy (XVII, 78). His right arm shattered by the bullet of a highwayman, Bullen delivers the gifts as Christmas Day dawns. "Tell him Sandy Claus has come," he says, before "fainting on the first threshold" (XVII, 79). The tale closes on this note of false pathos. Although it is written in Harte's "best vein of humor," as the *New York Evening Post* lamented, it is as "disappointing" as "The Poet of Sierra Flat" because "the catastrophe is far from being level with our expectations."[10] Henry James, who had met Harte at the Howells home, agreed the story was "better than anything in his 'second manner'—though not quite so good as his first."[11]

In addition to the 12 pieces printed in the two magazines, Harte wrote a melodramatic novella entitled "Mrs. Skaggs's Husbands" while under contract to Fields, Osgood. He apparently designed this two-part tale for serialization in the *Atlantic Monthly,* although, as Howells would conclude, "the long breath was not his" (*LFA,* 300). Osgood published the piece as the title story in a new collection of Harte's fiction in early 1873 and agreed to credit the author with the equivalent of "two articles for the 'Atlantic'" (*L,* 13). In the first part, set in the mining fields of central California, the young orphan Tommy Islington inherits the fortune of a wasted old miner known in camp as Johnson who, under the name Skaggs, had lost his wife and child, money, and reputation to another man back east 12 years before. After he discovers a cinnabar lode on his claim, Johnson disappears, apparently the victim of drowning, his body presumably washed out to sea. The irascible expressman Yuba Bill sends Tommy east "to finish his education" and admonishes him to "ferget every derned old spavined, string-halted bummer as you ever met or knew at Angel's,—ev'ry one, Tommy,—ev'ry one! (XVII, 30–31). (Shortly after completing this story, similarly, Harte insisted he was "not contemplating an early return to California,"[12] and he would eventually spurn an offer from Carmany to resume the editorship of the *Overland Monthly.*) Harte unfortunately resorts to caricature and contrivance to round out the story. In the second part, set 10 years later in the Eastern resort of Greyport (read, Newport), Tommy is a cultivated young gentleman, suitor to the hand of the fair Blanche Masterman. Yuba Bill unexpectedly appears to warn him that Johnson is not dead after all, but merely insane, and that he has come east to stalk the man who ruined his life. Coincidentally, Bill has briefly married the same "she-devil" who had been Johnson's wife. "There was days in that three months longer than any day in my life,—days, Tommy, when it was a toss-up whether I should kill her or she me," as he explains (XVII, 50). Predictably, Johnson appears on the scene, mistakes Bill for his old enemy Masterson and his own daughter Blanche for his former wife Mary, before losing his last vestige of sanity. The fortune he made in quicksilver will be restored to his blood-heir Blanche, it seems, by her imminent marriage to the heroic Tommy.

The fiction and poetry Harte wrote for Fields, Osgood quite simply failed to warrant a renewal of his contract when it expired in March 1872. "It was not his fault," Howells later wrote. Harte "was in the midst of new and alien conditions, and he had always his temperament against him, as well as the reluctant if not the niggard nature of his muse" (*LFA*, 301–302). Still, he was profoundly disappointed by this unexpected turn of events. When he sent the manuscript of "Concepcion de Arguëllo" to Howells on 19 March 1872, he invited the editor's suggestions. Howells took him at his word and posed a number of technical questions about the poem, which Harte was quick to resent. "Many thanks for your good-natured commendation of my ballad," he replied sarcastically on 25 March. "As to the corrections," he insisted he had consulted the standard historical sources available "in any public library" and punctuated the Spanish exactly as it was spoken: "I would trust my ear rather than my dictionary or the dicta of any set of Yankee Professors who give three syllables to 'Joaquin'" (Booth 1948, 328–29). Howells took umbrage at the tone of this letter and elicited an apology from Harte five days later, but the exchange epitomizes the strained relations between the editor and his former star contributor after the contract was allowed to lapse.

Itinerant Lecturer

Mark Twain claimed in 1907 that Harte "was an incorrigible borrower of money; he borrowed from all his friends; if he ever repaid a loan the incident failed to pass into history" (*MTE*, 272). The statement is a gross exaggeration. Harte was careless at best, irresponsible at worst, but he was no swindler. According to Noah Brooks, "he was continually involved in troubles that he might have escaped with a little more financial shrewdness."[13] Within weeks of losing his salary, unfortunately, Harte had run into debt. The first published reports of his chronic poverty began to circulate at the end of 1872. His former friend W. A. Kendall branded him a "loose and not infrequent borrower of considerable sums and then a cool ignorer of the gracious loaners."[14]

Harte tried to revive his failing fortunes, or capitalize on his waning reputation, by delivering a lecture entitled "The Argonauts of '49" in

Albany, Boston, New York, Washington, and Pittsburgh during the winter of 1872–73. He prefaced this loosely organized string of anecdotes about California in the 1850s with an announcement that "it was not all pretty, not instructive, perhaps not even true."[15] He compared the miners to Greek adventurers and the Gold Rush to the Crusades. As in his earlier letters from San Francisco to the *Christian Register* and *Springfield Republican,* he caricatured the exotic customs of gamblers and miners for his foreign audiences. "Some of the best men had the worst record," he averred, "and some of the worst rejoiced in a spotless Puritan pedigree."[16] He would, in fact, deliver this same address some 150 times over the next two years, from Montreal in the north and Macon, Georgia, in the south to Lawrence, Kansas, in the west (Stewart, 213–14). "I have traveled in the dead of winter from New York to Omaha 2,000 miles, with the thermometer varying from 10° to 25° below zero," he remembered later.[17] He even wrote a second lecture on "American Humor" with the obligatory testimonials to Twain, Artemus Ward, and Petroleum V. Nasby, which he read in both Chicago and New York during the 1874–75 season. By his own admission, however, he was something of a wooden orator, although his lectures were normally well-received. He reported to Fields on 18 December 1871, for example, that he had made a "decided hit" at Steinway Hall in New York two days before. "My agent is quietly informing the county lyceums, with a circular and notices, what they are losing," he added.[18] Overall, these performances were a mixed critical success and a financial fiasco. The receipts for his lecture at Tremont Temple in Boston on 13 December 1872 were seized at the behest of a creditor, and he suffered what he decorously termed "pecuniary failure" in Ottawa in March 1873. "There was scarcely enough money to pay expenses, and of course nothing to pay me with," as he explained to his wife (*L,* 20). He "suffered" other mortifying "failures" while on tour, moreover: the almost daily travel and repeated interruptions prevented him from writing (*L,* 310), and he returned from the Midwest in the spring of 1874 "nearly blind" with "inflamed eyes."[19] In the end, he was effectively fired by the James Redpath agency in 1875 for failing to honor some scheduled dates.[20]

Fragments Shored Against the Ruins

He was popularly compared at the time to "the stick which comes down in the dark after the rocket has gone up in a blaze of glory."[21]

Like Bartley Hubbard in *A Modern Instance*—to whom Howells would give Harte's initials if not his attributes—he tried desperately to reverse his slow descent into destitution. In November 1873 he moved his family to a "snug little house" in Morristown, New Jersey, which was "chiefly remarkable," or so he joked, for "being the only house" in town that "George Washington did not occupy as his headquarters during that dreadfully historical winter. . . . If the Father of his Country had resided here it might have changed his moral character. He could have told a lie without difficulty."[22] His name was still eminently bankable, more as a fiction writer than as a lecturer. In fact, he was paid liberally for the stories he contributed to the *New York Times* and *Scribner's* in 1873–74: "The *Times* paid me $600 for 'the Rose of Tuolumne,' $500 for '[A Passage in the Life of Mr.] John Oakhurst.' Scribner paid me $1,000 for '[An Episode of] Fiddletown'—16 pp. long and $500 for the 'Monte Flat Pastoral': 7 pp." Like a tailor paid for piecework, he labored over these months "to hawk my wares" (Booth 1948, 333) or "to finish some copy and get the shekels for it!"[23] Under the circumstances, he allowed the nexus of the market to dictate both the rate of production and the venue of publication. (He had, in scarcely two years, gone from the highest-salaried writer for the most prestigious magazine in America to free-lancing stories to the Sunday *feuilleton* of a daily screed.) "My stories have always been *contracted for, accepted* and the *prices fixed* before I had put pen to paper," he bragged to Howells, whom he chastised privately for breathing a rarefied "literary atmosphere which seems to exclude any vision of a broader literary world beyond,—its methods, profits and emoluments" (Booth 1948, 333).

On his part, Harte enthusiastically embraced that "broader literary world" by selling his "wares" to the highest bidder. Ever the vigilant editor, Howells tried to inspire him to raise his sights, although Harte scorned the suggestion. He blasted Howells in May 1874 for tinkering with the manuscript of his dramatic monologue "For the King," the first piece he placed in the *Atlantic* after the expiration of his contract, the poem he had given Osgood in an attempt to square their "little differences." "So little do I value the kind of criticism wh[ich] you have, I know in perfect goodness, indicated I might receive for these irregularities," he wrote the editor, "that I would have been perfectly satisfied had you printed the poem as I sent it" (Booth 1948, 332). He declined the invitation, floated by Howells only four months later, again to write exclusively for the *Atlantic Monthly* (albeit at a much lower salary than before). Their negotiations collapsed when Harte submitted the manuscript of his story "The Fool of Five Forks" to the magazine and received an offer of only $300 for it. "Since my arrival East," he carped, "I have never received so small an offer for any story." He withdrew the manuscript and sold it to the *New York Times* for $400. He obviously resented the "Yankee cheapening" of his banal poem "Ramon," for which he received but $125 upon its publication in the *Atlantic Monthly* for October 1874 (Booth 1948, 332–33). He admitted to Howells at the time that "I need the money,"[24] but he would not write for the magazine again. The next month, Howells acknowledged that his "Bret Harte negotiations" had fallen through but he had "more than made good the loss by securing Mark Twain for a series of sketches next year" (*LLWDH* I, 194). Twain would reminisce about his boyhood in Hannibal and his experiences as a riverboat pilot in "Life on the Mississippi"—in space in the *Atlantic Monthly* Harte might have claimed had he been less petulant.

To be sure, some of the tales he wrote for the *New York Times* and *Scribner's* during this period merit comparisons to his best fiction. He tried, if only intermittently, to work variations on his standard plot. "I am sick of my heroes of whatever genus—*homo* or *Ursa,* dying in an attitude on my hands," as he admitted to Mary Mapes Dodge (Booth 1944, 133–34). In "A Passage in the Life of Mr. John Oakhurst," first published in the *New York Times* for 28 June 1874, he both resurrected one of his most popular characters from the snowbank where he is buried at the end of "The Outcasts of Poker Flat" and inverted the formula of moral reformation he had used in such earlier gambler tales as "Outcasts" and "Brown of Calaveras." Oakhurst again plays against type through most of this story, refunding the poker losses of a fellow named Decker whose wife is a helpless invalid. She "had lost the use of her lower limbs from rheumatism" and "had tried many doctors, but without avail" (XVI, 47). Oakhurst is instantly smitten by this "pale, thin, deep-eyed woman" with her "shy virginity of manner" (XVI, 46). He invests in a resort hotel and arranges for her devoted if hapless husband to be hired there so that she can recover her health. When they meet at the springs two months later, Elsie Decker is transformed: this "graceful, shapely, elegantly attired gentlewoman" is again able to walk (XVI, 56). "You have re-created me," she tells Oakhurst. "You found a helpless, crippled, sick, poverty-stricken women, with one dress to her back, and that her own make, and you gave her life, health, strength, and fortune" (XVI, 57). To win her approval, Oakhurst stops gambling, sells his racehorses, attends church, shaves his moustache, dresses less garishly, loses his swagger, and takes a job as a stockbroker. Ironically, his rise to respectability is counterbalanced by Elsie Decker's moral decline. Despite her appearance of beauty, she has become a rapacious monster, a "cruel and selfish" *femme fatale* (XVI, 56) who carries on a secret affair with a banker even as she publicly flirts with Oakhurst. He learns the truth about the woman he loves only after he mortally wounds the banker in a duel fought (he thinks) to defend her honor. The tale ends on a note of ironic understatement as, two weeks later, a sadder but wiser Oakhurst returns to his old habits in the saloons of Sacramento. Like "Mrs. Skaggs's Husbands," this story is a thinly veiled satire of marriage, and it was written shortly before the author began to drop hints of his own marital problems. "[I]n California I used to ride a mule," he recalled in a letter to the poet Mary E. W. Sherwood in October 1875. "That probably prevented me from marrying an heiress. It was a mule that eventually delivered me into the hands of Mrs. Harte."[25]

Whereas "Plain Language from Truthful James" failed as a satire of racism because its subtleties were misunderstood, "Wan Lee, the Pagan," in *Scribner's* for September 1874, was utterly unambiguous in its indictment of race hatred. According to Duckett, "Harte's most effective means of combating race prejudice against Chinese was creating individual Chinese characters who, because their ways seemed no longer dark or inscrutable, became likable fellow human beings with strong claims to the reader's sympathy" (Duckett 1957, 256). The narrator introduces the reader in the opening paragraphs of this tale to a "grave, decorous, handsome" Chinese gentleman whose character revises the prevailing Oriental stereotype: "His manner was urbane" and he "spoke French and English fluently" (XVI, 82). This patriarch apprentices the impish child Wan Lee to the narrator, a newspaperman in Humboldt County, when his life is threatened by "the younger members" of the "Christian and highly civilized race" who "attend the enlightened schools in San Francisco" (XVI, 89). Two years later, the narrator takes a job in the city and Wan Lee, although wary of the move, soon befriends a young neighbor there, a girl he "worshipped" with "something of the same superstition, but without any of the caprice, that he bestowed upon his porcelain Pagan god" (XVI, 101). The entire tale to this point is merely preface to its final page; that is, Harte has written this "true story" (XVI, 102) so that he can end it on a pathetic note. "There were two days of that eventful year which will long be remembered in San Francisco," Harte writes in his own voice, "when a mob of her citizens set upon and killed unarmed, defenceless foreigners because they were foreigners, and of another race, religion, and color, and worked for what wages they could get" (XVI, 102–3). No puzzling references here to how "we" are "ruined by Chinese cheap labor." Wan Lee, an innocent victim of mindless violence, is stoned to death by "a mob of half-grown boys and Christian schoolchildren" (XVI, 104).

Gabriel Conroy

Harte was a miniaturist whose skill at portraiture did not translate easily to a large canvas. Or as Howells observed, he "could not write a novel, though he produced the like of one" (*LFA,* 300). He had, in fact, contracted to write a three-volume story for the American Publishing Co. of Hartford, a subscription press, in September 1872. By June 1874, when he finally began to work on the story, his $1,000 advance had long since evaporated and he was hounded by creditors. Within a month, he was complaining to his publisher Elisha Bliss that "the mere labor of writing" the prologue was "withering. But as I have to dispose of my characters so as to use them advantageously in the remaining 'Books'—it is the hardest work I have done." He ended his letter with a characteristic plea for money: "Meanwhile how am I to live? I've been a month at 50 pp." (Booth 1944, 135). Although he confessed in September that he was "usually so far in the rearward of my promises to the printer that they generally lie in wait for each sheet as it leaves my lagging pen,"[26] he soon increased his production of "copy" to 1,000 words a day. By the following March, he admonished Bliss that "I am writing a great deal faster than you are printing and you are about 300 pp. behind. Do hurry up!"[27] In all, Harte collected $3,400 in metered advances as he worked on the novel over the next 11 months. For example, when he sent Bliss the last chapters of book 5 in January 1875 he reported he had "drawn upon you for $75—as I am in need of money, and have just given up ½ dozen lecture engagements [the cancellations that prompted Redpath to fire him?] to keep at this work. It ought to pay me eventually for it certainly doesn't now."[28] That same month, ironically, he was forced to deny publicly a rumor that he had "obtained, through influential friends," a salaried post in the New York Custom House "as a relief from pecuniary embarrassment." (Had the report been true, he would have become Herman Melville's coworker there.) "I have always found my profession sufficiently lucrative," he asserted.[29] When the lyceum lecturer Anna Dickinson met him by chance in New York in March, however, she reported that he looked very ill. If the "poor fellow" could only be "put into a great library & be fed & clothed, & have all his worldly wants supplied, & be allowed to write & work unrestricted & unhampered he would do what is *in* him to do but will never now come out of him" (Young, 45). Fortunately, *Scribner's* purchased serial rights to the novel—entitled *Gabriel Conroy* because, Harte thought, "the shorter the title, the better the chance for its quotation and longevity" (*L,* 50)—sight unseen in May 1875 for a record $6,000, divided equally between the author and publisher.[30] Still, their relations deteriorated over the months because, Bliss claimed, Harte was submitting ever-briefer chapters in order to collect his advances at ever-briefer intervals. "Now don[']t say anything again about my installments being short," he replied. "I am working exclusively upon the novel, and depend upon these remittances promptly."[31] By October 1875 he was again "short of funds" and in debt to Lord & Taylor's for about $1,100. His comment to Osgood on his predicament resounds with the unmistakable accent of self-pity: "I have done all a poor man, with a large family, can do toward settling a debt that he cannot pay outright."[32] He pinned/penned great hopes on the book, and it remained a personal favorite among all his works to the end of his life.

It was not, however, very good. More to the point, it betrays the haste with which it was written. In "construction *Gabriel Conroy* is indeed from beginning to end hopelessly and irredeemably bad," the *Saturday Review* scolded.[33] Harte stuffed the panoramic story like an old sofa, with sufficient plots and subplots to fill a small library, most of these complications pivoting upon incredible coincidences and resolved by convulsions of nature or revelations of mistaken identity. The story opens upon a starving band of emigrants—including the adolescent Gabriel Conroy, his sister Grace, and the apparently virtuous Philip Ashley, whose real name is Arthur Poinsett—snowbound in the Sierras like the legendary Donner party. Philip and Grace set out to find help, floating downriver on a tree. As they approach a settlement, Philip convinces the beautiful 14-year-old Grace to impersonate his sister in order to avoid the appearance of impropriety while he returns with some men to the mountains. Incredibly, it turns out later that Philip is altogether too sensitive on this score: he has seduced Grace and gotten her with child during their several days together. She then disappears from the novel for a few hundred pages. Meanwhile, another party of men stumbles by chance across the remaining emigrants stranded in the mountains. These rescuers ignore the evidence of cannibalism among the party and bury a body they presume to be that of Grace. Some five years later, the "plain, unostentatious, powerful giant" Gabriel (*GC,* I, 254)—a character modeled, according to Anna Harte, upon her husband[34]—discovers a rich silver mine on the land where he builds his cabin. Grace, of course, would have a claim to this wealth as his sister. She also has been deeded the property by a Dr. Devarges, a botanist and one of the original emigrants who died in the snow. But she is presumed to be dead, an assumption that plunges the narrative into a labyrinthine subplot about a mysterious Mexican and his mistress, Devarges's widow Julie, who tries to defraud Gabriel with a forged document, impersonates Grace to claim the land, and finally marries Gabriel for his money. As the reviewer for the *Times* of London noted, this "female fiend" is "in the habit of breaking the seventh and eighth Commandments, and is awkwardly mixed up in a breach of the sixth."[35] When Gabe realizes he has been duped, the gentle if stupid giant signs all his worldly belongings over to the devious minx, who suddenly realizes that she really loves him. When the mysterious Mexican is killed, Gabriel is arrested for the murder. He refuses to contest the charge, believing that his wife is the guilty party. (In fact, the fellow committed suicide by falling on his back onto his knife.) Gabriel is the victim of idle rumormongering—much like the author at the time he was writing the story—and he is saved from a lynch mob only by the timely intervention of Jack Hamlin. Grace—who, of course, is not dead after all—reappears to testify at her brother's trial. Her skin has been indelibly stained brown with dye so she can pass as the adopted daughter and heiress of the late Commander of San Ramon. As Doña Dolores, she has a prior claim under the old Spanish land grants to the mine her brother owns, whereupon Harte rehabilitates the scoundrel Ashley who, although he had failed to recognize Grace in the course of several interviews with Doña Dolores, has never forgotten her. All of the lovers—Ashley and Grace, Julie and Gabe—are soon reconciled and, on the last page of a novel with more loose ends than a frayed rope, Our Hero has even discovered a second silver mine.

This disjointed and episodic story was, predictably, scorned roundly by the critics. The *Illustrated London News* complained it was "told in so desultory a manner and with such a superabundance of characters" that readers lose interest "long before the last chapter."[36] The *Athe-*

naeum dismissed it as "Bret Harte without the invigorating freshness of his native California airs."[37] Harte's old friends at the *Springfield Republican* pronounced it "a moral and literary failure of uncommon magnitude and offensiveness."[38] Horace Scudder opined in the *Atlantic Monthly* that "all the dark passages through which [the reader] has been wandering" in this book lead finally "not into the light, but into the vegetable cellar."[39] More recently, Richard O'Connor dismissed it as "an episodic grab-bag, a catchall with everything but a firm and consistent story-line."[40] Yet the novel passed through no fewer than 14 editions in two German translations—it was "the book upon which my literary reputations rests in Germany," as Harte wrote Osgood in 1880.[41] And James Joyce, no less, would model "The Dead" at least in part upon it, even naming one of his characters Gabriel Conroy.[42] But Harte's "breakthrough" novel was, in the end, no less a commercial than a critical flop. Bliss concluded prior to publication that he had bought a pig in a poke, a subscription book whose "value had almost disappeared" (*MTE*, 281). While Harte's contract specified that he would accrue a modest royalty, he would never so much as receive a formal statement on his account with the publisher. In fact, he expressed repeated doubts about Bliss's honesty during the summer of 1877, when he desperately needed any money owed him. He eventually urged Osgood to buy rights to the novel from the American Publishing Co. and reprint it: "The book has never had a fair show in America—through its infelicitous birth in Hartford." Bliss simply claimed "that the expenses and advances have or *had*—for it is nearly three years since I wrote to them—not yet been covered by sales or royalties."[43] He was outraged to learn, in 1884, that Bliss had sold the dramatic rights to the story to a theatrical producer without even consulting him. In retrospect, Harte's misgivings seem perfectly justified. As of August 1896, his account with the press was still more than $4,000 in arrears—more than he had received in total advances while writing the novel—and Houghton Mifflin bought the copyright the next year for a mere $350.[44]

Two Men of Sandy Bar

Harte once wrote "a play which would have succeeded if anyone else had written it," or so Twain recalled in 1907. After the play opened to a chorus of disparaging reviews, however, he "earned the enmity of the New York dramatic critics by freely and frequently charging them with being persons who never said a favorable thing about a new play except when the favorable thing was bought and paid for beforehand" (*MTE*, 275). Throughout its run at the Union Square Theatre in late August and September 1876, Harte's *Two Men of Sandy Bar* was a source of controversy, a dramatic *cause célèbre* that centered less upon its merits as a play than upon the integrity of the playwright and the critics he accused of corruption. This episode illustrates, more than any other in his long career, the extent to which Harte became a creature of the marketplace.

Harte had long harbored the ambition to write for the stage, although he would prove in the end to be rather inept at it. As a child of 12, he once claimed, he had written a play in which "Gilded Vice was triumphant and Simple Virtue and Decent Respectability suffered through five acts."[45] In the summer of 1870, even before leaving California, he agreed—for $2,500 down and $100 per performance—to script a play for Lawrence Barrett entitled "In the Sierras," which would depict the principal characters from his stories.[46] In mid–March 1871, barely a week after contracting to contribute his poems and sketches exclusively to the publishers of the *Atlantic,* he opened negotiations with the impresario Augustin Daly to write another play.[47] In June 1872, shortly after the expiration of his contract with Fields, Osgood, Harte agreed with Daly to write "a play in five acts suitable for the Fifth Avenue Theatre," said script to be "completely finished" within 90 days (Felheim, 296). Two years later, he was still working, with Dion Boucicault, on a scenario entitled "Kentuck," apparently about the character by that name who had appeared in "The Luck of Roaring Camp." Their collaboration was not a happy one, however. As Boucicault reported to Daly, Harte "is very anxious to get the work done—but thinks we can scurry over the ground more rapidly than is consistent with safety."[48] As Harte would later admit, "I can write dialogue like an angel, draw character like a heaven-born genius, but I can't make *situations* and *plots*" (*L,* 213). As if to prove the point, he wrote three separate sections of *Gabriel Conroy* in dramatic form. Each of these early projects mercifully died of natural causes.

With the end of his novel in sight in the spring of 1875, however, Harte agreed to write a comedy for the actor Stuart Robson for about $6,000—$3,000 in advance and $50 per performance during its first season on stage—and he moved with his family to Cohasset, Massachusetts, to be near both Robson and Barrett.[49] He wrote Osgood that "I have got tired of enriching only publishers" (*L,* 51), and the *New*

York Evening Post reported that the price was "not perhaps altogether out of proportion to the reputation of the author."[50] Annie Fields wrote in her diary in September 1875 that Harte "evidently enjoyed [his work on] the play" in anticipation of "the fame and the money" he expected it to bring him (Howe, 243). Nevertheless, he soon regretted his failure to strike a better deal. He wrote Twain in January 1876 that he feared he had been "a tremendous fool" for selling rights to the play "as I did" because, of course, he expected it to be a hit (Duckett 1964, 98). From all indications, *Two Men of Sandy Bar* was little more than an elaborate revision of Harte's old script "In the Sierras." He cannibalized the plot from two of his California yarns, "Mr. Thompson's Prodigal" and "The Idyl of Red Gulch"—a critical mistake on which years later he blamed the "failure" of the melodrama (Booth 1944, 140–41). He added, solely for comic effect, a "heathen Chinee" laundryman named Hop Sing. Harte swelled the cast by adding a character designed to be played by Robson—Colonel Culpepper Starbottle, the Southern pettyfogger who had earlier figured in the stories "Brown of Calaveras" and "The Iliad of Sandy Bar." The stage role was no doubt inspired by the recent success of Colonel Sellers, the hero of Twain's comedy *The Gilded Age.* Harte estimated that his original script, before he began to prune its overgrowth, "would play about 4-1/4 hours."[51] Boucicault told him *Two Men of Sandy Bar* "contained material for half-a-dozen plays" (Pemberton, 260) and, in fact, the scenario is so convoluted as to defy brief synopsis.

The two men of the title are John Oakhurst and Sandy Morton, the first a gambler, the other a drunk. Oakhurst loves the proud Mexican beauty Jovita, for whom Morton works; on his part, Morton thinks he is married to the Duchess, a sexual temptress who left him for Oakhurst and who has deceived both of them: she has never divorced her first husband, to whom she eventually returns after leaving with Sandy the child she has borne to their union. In scene two, the rich banker Alexander Morton arrives at Jovita's rancho with Starbottle, his legal advisor, in search of his prodigal son Sandy, whereupon the gambler assumes the identity of the younger Morton—and here the first of four acts ends. Harte has, in a sense, allegorized his own financial plight in the play: the two men of Sandy Bar are economic competitors, claimants to the same birthright. Like Oakhurst, who poses as a dutiful son over the course of a year to win old Morton's confidence, Harte had tried to prove his worth during the year he wrote under contract to Fields, Osgood. Much as Oakhurst ignores the beautiful Jovita while he lives in Morton's mansion, however, Harte had neglected his craft. Like Sandy, moreover, he has become a hired menial, a victim of the impersonal market. In the final act, Harte imagines an ideal solution to his problems: Oakhurst repents and proposes marriage to Jovita (Harte's California subject); Sandy reforms and falls in love with an Eastern schoolma'am (Harte's genteel audience); and both men are reconciled with the elder Morton, who names them partners in his banking house.[52] Incredibly, the role of Starbottle, played by Robson, was entirely superfluous to this tangle of plots, and the most amusing of the characters—Hop Sing, played by the Anglo actor C. T. Parsloe—appeared on stage for little more than five minutes and delivered a total of only nine lines.

Predictably, such a pastiche, produced in the summer and fall of 1876 in Chicago, New York, Hartford, Washington, and Baltimore, was mostly panned by reviewers. After a somewhat abbreviated version of the play opened in Chicago in mid-July, the critic for the *Chicago Tribune* opined that the script betrayed "serious faults" of design and "evidences of carelessness and slipshod writing," although he was heartened to learn "the obnoxious last act is to be overhauled altogether" and some of the dialogue "ruthlessly compressed."[53] The critic for the *Chicago Inter-Ocean* thought the play "the work of a clever amateur" and compared it to an "ill-fitting garment" requiring alterations.[54] Leonard Glover, manager of the Adelphi Theatre in Chicago, tried to tinker with the script but, as he privately admitted, "I was forced to the conclusion that little could be done to mend it. . . . [T]o give S[andy] B[ar] any considerable dramatic importance would require three or four of the characters to be wholly rewritten, which might make a very bad play of what, at present, the public seem to consider very good nonsense."[55] The next month, despite slight revisions in the play, the New York reviewers were not so tactful as their counterparts in Chicago. The *New York Times,* for example, carped that Harte had written, not a script, but a "nondescript," and condemned *Two Men of Sandy Bar* as "the worst failure witnessed on the boards of our theatres for years, . . . the most dismal mass of trash that was ever put into dramatic shape before a New York audience." Robson had, in effect, been swindled: "He has paid an enormous sum for a piece of writing that has not a scintilla of wit, nor the slightest degree of literary merit."[56] William Winter, drama critic of the *New York Tribune* and one of the first Eastern critics to champion Harte's work, was "generally adverse to the piece,"[57] and a wag at the *New York Herald* suggested that the play resembled "one of Beadle's dime novels struck by light-ning."[58] The critics for the *New York Evening Post* and *Commercial Advertiser* were scarcely more complimentary.[59] Brander Matthews complained the play had "no singleness of purpose—no definite aim."[60] Only A. C. Wheeler of the *New York World* qualified his criticism by praising the "bright, clever, dexterous and fresh" plot, and Harte wrote Wheeler the same day the notice appeared to thank him for it: "It is the only one that the 'Two Men of Sandy Bar' has received, wherein the writer shows that he is able to exercise his judgement as a critic without losing his respect for himself, his Art, or the subject he criticizes."[61] In all, the play was so maligned in the New York press that Boucicault issued a public denial that he had had any part in writing it.[62]

Rather than withdraw the farce, Harte foolishly rose to its defense. His motives were largely venal: in 1866, as he remembered, Edwin Forrest had performed nightly for an entire month before packed houses in San Francisco after local critics began by turns to assail and defend his acting style (*BHC,* 46). Harte seems to have adopted a similar strategy to publicize his play and offset the negative reviews. He derided the New York drama critics in a self-serving letter to the editor of the *New York Herald*—a letter that announces the title of the play, the theatre where it was appearing, and the name of its star in the first sentence: "If I did not at once apologize in the public journals for the perpetration and production of a play entitled 'Two Men of Sandy Bar,' at the Union Square Theatre last Monday night," he wrote, "it was because I received a letter from Mr. Stuart Robson" who assured him that the script answered his "fullest expectations as an actor." Robson had anticipated the critics' slurs, he claimed, because in New York "the largest purse command[s] the longest and strongest" theatrical reviews; as a result, some of the most "abused plays of recent production have been the best received by the public and the most lasting successes" on the boards. (In other words, critics are known to take bribes.) "I have not yet seen the play, having been absent from town," Harte allowed, "but I shall take an early opportunity to do so. If I find it half as bad as my most friendly critics have alleged I shall probably abandon it to this most unfortunate and infatuated man [Robson], and in my functions as a critic, I doubt not, shall now and then castigate it as his property. But if, on the other hand, I shall find that my critics are prejudiced, envious, ignorant or mistaken, why, I may demand through your friendly columns to be tried by a jury of my peers."[63] If

Harte intended to excite controversy in hopes of saving the play, his plan seems to have succeeded, if only temporarily. For several days after this letter appeared, the Union Square Theatre was filled for each performance.[64]

Certainly Harte's needle touched a nerve. The next day, the *New York Tribune* dismissed both Robson's "exceedingly foolish letter" and Harte's "particularly ill-bred and mendacious indorsement" of it,[65] and the *New York Evening Post* called on the actor or author to "give the facts" if either of them "knows any critic belonging to any respectable journal in this city" who had attempted blackmail.[66] Over the next few days, both the *New York Sun,* edited by Harte's friend Charles A. Dana, and the *New York Commercial Advertiser* also urged him to name names.[67] After the *New York Sun,* on 9 September, published an explicit claim by Robson's agent that he had been offered "the favorable opinions of at least one of the journals of New York" for a price, the *New York World* entered the fray by again demanding "the name of the person who made such an offer."[68] The proverbial ball was in Harte's court, and he volleyed by firing off a second letter, published in Dana's *New York Sun,* in which he suggested that any local journalists offended by his remarks sue him for libel:

I have been called upon by the various journals of the city to give the names of certain critics connected with the New York press, whom Mr. Robson, in a letter to me about "Two Men of Sandy Bar," charges with bribery and corruption. Generally, I believe, it is the utterer and not the receiver of an alleged counterfeit who is called upon to make his tender good. . . . As to the names asked for, one has already been given to an influential journal of this city. . . . If, however, further names and proofs are demanded, they can be evoked from me simply and readily. It is difficult to get a manager or actor to admit that they have paid for favorable critical services, but they may be obliged to testify under due process of law. An action for libel would call out the proof; but as I cannot bring such an action, not being able to conscientiously swear that the expression of these critics has damaged me or my play, I would propose that those gentlemen who are aggrieved by my charges should bring an action against me. . . . [69]

Of course, no charge of libel was brought against Harte for the simple reason that he had mentioned no names. He had no legal exposure on which such a suit could be filed.

His second letter had raised the stakes, however. The *New York Evening Post* denounced it as a "cowardly" evasion of the issue,[70] and the

New York Dramatic News launched an investigation into the affair. A stringer for the *New York World*—ironically, the New York paper which had been least critical of the play and whose reviewer Harte had privately thanked—denied in a statement to the *Sun* that he was the blackmailer.[71] Meanwhile, the *World* censured Harte and Robson editorially and concluded that "it is not the repute of the dramatic critics of New York which is in question, but the good faith of the authors of this tempest in a teapot."[72] Unfortunately, this editorial elicited from Harte yet another letter, this one published in both the scandal sheet *New York Daily Graphic* and the low-class *New York Evening Mail,* in which he struck out like a cornered animal. The *World* had been notified that "one of its own employes" was the corrupt critic "who criticized my play," he asserted, "but the name of the critic and, what was more important to the public, the name of the paper, were studiously concealed." Lest the allegations in his earlier letters seem too general, Harte charged that the editors of *World* had allowed "a critic who demanded money from an actor to afterwards write the criticism for their columns" and had been apprised of "these facts," yet publicly denied them. "It seems to me that this charge, if false, is actionable, and that the *World* could readily bring such action against me."[73]

Most New York papers chose simply to ignore this latest diatribe, although a few journals held Harte up to ridicule and the *World* published a rebuttal the next day.[74] The *New York Clipper* joked that Harte and Robson "have succeeded in working up a very lively discussion about the merits of 'The Two Men of Sandy Bar,' and in their way have secured a good deal of cheap advertising, which ought to successfully carry the two men through the country without any bar."[75] The *Nation* avowed that "no candid person" who had attended a performance of the play "would ever dream of any self-respecting critic speaking well" of it "without a large bonus of ready money paid in advance. Knowing that this precaution had not been taken," Harte had naturally assumed "that the absence of the favorable criticism was due to the non-payment of the money."[76] In late September, the play completed its five-week run at the Union Square Theatre as originally scheduled, although in the end it was nearly as great a commercial and critical failure as *Gabriel Conroy.* Three days after it closed, Harte wrote Osgood to arrange for its publication as a book and to ask for "an advance of $150. Send me your cheque—that's a good fellow. I am in want of money. Then go on and sell 2 or 3,000 copies at $1.00 each."[77] Better a well-paid than a well-made play, or so it seems.

Harte's already spotty reputation was indelibly tarnished by the controversy, moreover. Charles Dudley Warner gossiped about "the row Bret has had with the critics about his play" in a letter to C. H. Webb in October. Warner did not attempt to disguise his own sympathies in the matter: "The play is poorly acted," he wrote, and Harte's script "pretty lame."[78] Publicly, Howells rallied to Harte's side, declaring (albeit anonymously) in the *Atlantic Monthly* that, while he had not seen the play, he was certain it had "failed through the malice of enemies furious at having offered themselves for sale in vain."[79] Privately, however, Howells thought Harte had "acted crazily about the criticism of his play" (*MT–HL* I, 162). Wheeler of the *New York World* threatened to resign from the staff of the paper as late as January 1877 "in consequence of some disagreement" with his editors that grew out of Harte's charges.[80] Harte apparently fell so far behind on his rent in Cohasset, meanwhile, that Lawrence Barrett paid it "to avoid appearing in an unpleasant controversy over bills."[81] On his part, Robson took *Two Men of Sandy Bar* on the road, first to Baltimore and Washington, where he assured Harte "I will soon get back the $6,000 the dignified 'Times' says you swindled me out of."[82] Robson kept the farce in his repertoire for at least two seasons, although in a production of it in San Francisco in September 1878 he did not assume the part of Starbottle, the role Harte had written for him, but the part of the drunkard Sandy Morton. In one crucial respect, however, nothing had changed: the play still was panned by the critics.[83]

Ah Sin

Only one person who ever saw a performance of *Two Men of Sandy Bar* in New York seems to have wholeheartedly enjoyed it: the author's old friend Mark Twain. "Harte's play can be doctored till it will be entirely acceptable & then it will clear a great sum every year," he wrote Howells. "The play entertained me hugely, even in its present crude state" (*MT–HL* I, 152). He had particularly enjoyed Hop Sing, a "perfectly delightful" (*MTE*, 275) and "wonderfully funny creature" (*MT–HL* I, 157). When Harte proposed that they write a play together "& divide the swag," Twain leapt at the chance. Each of them would "draw a plot" and they would then use "the best of the two, or gouge from both & build a third." Harte would "put in" the lead, an Oriental type who would again be acted by Parsloe, though "both of us will work on him & develop him" (*MT–HL* I, 157). On so flimsy a basis

began the most ill-fated collaboration in the history of American letters. Only three weeks before, ironically, Harte had expressed the fear
"the Chinaman" would "become tiresome and monotonous as the central figure in a three-act play."[84] As it happened, his hunch was right.

The product of their collaboration, *Ah Sin,* was another low comedy
of mistaken identity, its dialogue an unhappy marriage of Western
drawl and pidgin English. As finally produced, the play was mostly
Twain's—he wrote Howells at the time that he had "left hardly a foot-
print of Harte" in the script (*MT–HL* I, 192), although he elsewhere
allowed that Harte's "part of it was the best part" (*MTE,* 278). Set in
the Stanislaus region of central California, the plot is vaguely reminiscent of Harte's "A Monte Flat Pastoral," first published in *Scribner's* for
January 1874, though the irony and pathos of the original story have
been sacrificed to farce. The villain Broderick, after tossing the hapless
victim Pluckett off a cliff, frames the hero, Henry York, for the murder. On his part, York confuses the genteel wife and daughter of Judge
Tempest, a wealthy San Franciscan, with the vulgar relatives of Plunkett. At York's trial before the local vigilance committee, Miss Tempest reveals her true identify and confesses her love for Our Hero. Ah
Sin presents evidence to convict Broderick of the crime, when suddenly
Old Man Plunkett appears to prove he is not really dead after all.

As contrived as *Ah Sin* may now seem, Harte and Twain were confident it would be a hit. The play opened in Washington to modestly
favorable notices in May 1877 and, Twain reported, it was "a-booming
at the Fifth Avenue" theatre in New York in early August (*MT–HL* I,
177, 191). The *New York Herald* thought it could make "two or three"
fortunes and predicted for it "a long run."[85] On 20 August, Harte
wrote that his play was "a sort of success," a property at least "valuable
enough for Parsloe to try and buy" his share of it. Although financially
hard-pressed, he refused to sell.[86] His money sense was, as usual, dead
wrong. By October, the play had folded like a poker player with a
losing hand. It was, in the end, "a most abject & incurable failure"
(*MT–HL,* I, 206). As Frederick Anderson has remarked, "While *Ah
Sin* is not the poorest work by either man, it is not far from it" (*AS,*
v). Neither Harte nor Twain would include it in his collected works.
Indeed, the play was lost until a prompt copy of it surfaced among
Daly's papers and was published in a limited edition in 1961. Not only
had their collaboration failed, moreover, their friendship had ended for
a variety of reasons. Among them: Harte believed Twain, who held an

interest in the American Publishing Co., had conspired to bilk him on the sales of *Gabriel Conroy*. He had also asked Twain for a loan and been refused. Instead, Twain had offered him $25 a week and board to help him write another play. Harte contemptuously declined in a letter signaling an irrevocable break in their relations. He resented Twain's attempt to exploit "my poverty" and concluded: "As a shrewd man, a careful man, a provident man, I think you will admit that in my circumstances the writing of plays with you is not profitable" (Duckett 1964, 136).

"That *Awful, Terrible Last Winter*"

Although he was normally a painstaking and even fastidious writer, Harte's work habits in the mid– to late 1870s, under financial pressure and the strain of a failing marriage, were increasingly slipshod. Charles Warren Stoddard remembered that, in the old *Overland Monthly* days, Harte would pace the floor while "waiting for a word, the right word, the one word of all others to fit into a line of recently written prose."[87] In order to cash in on the Centennial craze in late 1876, however, Harte wrote the last half of the story "Thankful Blossom"—which contains about 20,000 words in all—in the course of a single night and drank two quarts of whiskey besides (*MTE,* 275–76). Set in Morristown, New Jersey, during the American Revolution, this tale of intrigue in the Continental Army recounts Miss Thankful's conversion (à la J. W. De Forest's Civil War novel) from Toryism to Patriotism. Her shifting sympathies are signaled by her change of lovers, from the traitorous Captain Brewster of the Connecticut Contingent to the dashing and loyal Major Van Zandt. Although Twain believed the story "belongs at the very top of Harte's literature" (*MTE,* 276) and the *San Francisco Chronicle* thought the heroine of this "charming" tale was "as odd and piquant as her name,"[88] the *Boston Advertiser* griped that the ancillary characters were "sketched rapidly."[89] (As Harte portrayed him, George Washington is as wooden as his teeth.) The *New York World*—scarcely inclined to praise the author after the *Two Men of Sandy Bar* contretemps—settled an old score in its notice: the romance "is even more 'bobtailed' than 'Gabriel Conroy,'" the reviewer grumbled. "It is an open question as to what improvement in Mr. Harte's style would be wrought by his reduction to a state of abject penury; but the experiment of ruining him is worth trying. At present, there is no author who seems so set upon losing a reputation honorably won as Mr. Harte, and we make no doubt that after two or three more books like this he will prove successful."[90]

Harte hoped to arrest the downward spiral of his career when, in the summer of 1877, he was invited to edit a new weekly magazine called *The Capital* to be published by Donn Piatt in Washington, D.C. Piatt offered him either a flat annual salary of $5,000 or $3,000 plus a one-half interest in the journal, and Harte opted for the latter. "Washington is the place for a literary man to make money," he declared (*L,* 56). Although "some newspaper men," including Dana, warned him privately that no "Washington paper can succeed," he was "satisfied to try." If the venture turned a profit, he would earn "money, and reputation, and self-respect." As a precaution, however, he instructed his lawyers to draft an agreement to shield him "from any indebtedness of the Company over and above my share in it" if it fails.[91] Despite some nagging health problems, he wrote a serial that summer for the magazine entitled "The Story of a Mine." "It isn't a bad story," he protested, and "some of it has been written in the sorest trouble I have ever had" (*L,* 61). Harte thought it had topical appeal: "It is essentially adapted to the times, and the business depression."[92] Unfortunately, like his other best-laid plans, the magazine project fell through. "Piatt could not fulfill his promise" in the end, and the company collapsed under a mountain of debt before the first issue appeared. Even the money Harte was promised for his story was seized by Piatt's creditors. "I have had no money since I have been here," he wrote Anna from Washington on September 21. His wife was "alone, penniless," stranded in a "strange hotel" in New York (*L,* 60–62). "I would have returned each night," he poignantly confessed, "but for the expense and the certainty that my presence there without money would only provoke my creditors. God knows how you are getting on—I dare not think!"[93]

He supported his family through the winter of his discontent by writing a series of banal poems and thin articles—some of them even unsigned—for *Godey's,* the *New York Times,* and the *New York Sun* and borrowing money from his friend Dana. One of these squibs, "The Hoodlum Band," presumably parodies dime novels, although it is scarcely distinguishable from the pulp fiction it burlesques. Another story, entitled "Jinny," is the highly romanticized biography of a California mule. Yet a third piece, "The Man Whose Yolk Was Not Easy," is a black humor account of the final days in the life of a former soldier "afflicted with an aneurism caused by the buckle of his knapsack pressing upon the arch of the aorta" (I, 223), a trope for the author's own predicament. Harte's reputation, meanwhile, suffered another hemorrhage of sorts. In January 1878, the pseudononymous New York correspondent of the *Cincinnati Gazette* quoted one of his "best friends"— no doubt his former collaborator Mark Twain—to the effect that "Harte was absolutely devoid of a conscience. If his washerwoman had saved $500 by long years of careful industry, he would borrow it without the slightest intention of repaying it."[94] The item was widely copied around the country, much to Harte's chagrin. Little wonder he wrote at the time that "[t]here is an indescribable delicacy in the legal profession which we literary folk ought to imitate" (XVIII, 345). Years later he reflected upon "that nervousness that daily bent me" and his "shiftless, hand-to-mouth life" during that "very bitter winter,"[95] "that *awful, terrible last winter*" in America (*L,* 115), the very nadir of his career. "I could not, and *would not under any circumstances,*" he declared, "again go through what I did in New York the last two years and particularly the last winter I passed there" (*L,* 308).

"The Story of a Mine" finally appeared as a book published by Osgood in February 1878. It was an experiment of sorts, the putative history of a quicksilver mine from its discovery through the resolution of its legal status by Congressional inaction. Its cast of characters constantly changes as the scene shifts from the Coast Range of California to the financial district of San Francisco to the Capitol in Washington. Harte wrote part of chapter 6 as a dramatic dialogue, a distracting earmark of his style in mid-and late career. Although it is nearly twice as long as "Thankful Blossom," the story gathers momentum only in its final chapters, which satirize lobbyists and federal bureaucrats much as Dickens lampooned the Circumlocution Office in *Little Dorrit* and Twain political corruption in *The Gilded Age.* Washington City "was a capital of Contradictions and Inconsistencies," Harte wrote, and "the crowning Inconsistency was that, from time to time, it was submitted to the sovereign people to declare if these various Inconsistencies were not really the perfect expression of the most perfect Government the world had known" (XVIII, 380, 382). He caricatured Charles Sumner of Massachusetts in the person of "an eminent and respected" if pompous Senator who represents "a scholarly, orderly, honorable, and radical Commonwealth" (XVIII, 442). Ironically, the dead weight of this Senator's reputation thwarts the attempted land grab of Congressman Gashwiler, the "King of Misrule and the Lord of the Unfinished Business" (XVIII, 459). In dismissing the tale as "incoherent and feeble" the *Literary World* merely expressed the prevailing critical opinion.[96] M. W. Hazeltine tactfully allowed in the *New York Sun* that "Harte is not over circumspect or happy in the concatenation of its plot."[97] Even Harte once disparaged it as a "wretched story" (*L, 63*). As Stewart suggests, the piece was "stillborn" from his pen and colored "like a dingy fog" by his despair (Stewart, 241). In May 1878, the *Boston Traveller* quipped that Harte was "floating on the raft made of the shipwreck of his former reputation."[98]

He was reduced, in the end, to trivial hackwork to stave off his creditors. For $50, he parodied Longfellow's "Excelsior" in an advertisement for Sapolio soap.[99] In the spring of 1878, he wrote a plodding 400-line jingle entitled "Cadet Grey" for a humor book entitled *West Point Tic Tacs* and endured the indignities of a literal-minded editor who quibbled with some of his references to military protocol. But, as he admitted, "I have given up my other work for this and am behind in my income."[100] Even before the publication of "The Story of a Mine" in February, he sent Osgood some additional "copy" and took umbrage at the firm's apparent "tardiness" in accepting it. "Do you think you are treating me exactly right?" he queried Osgood after only three weeks. "I am anxious to know if this lengthy consideration of my proposition is to be taken as a form of declining, and if I am to have the privilege of trying my luck with another publisher."[101]

Meanwhile, he angled for a diplomatic post in the grand tradition of Irving, Lowell, Hawthorne, and Howells. According to Twain, in fact, Harte claimed he had been promised a foreign consulate by both Presidential candidates in the election of 1876 (*MTE, 287*). However, after William Evarts denied his application to join the China Mission, as Harte noted, "every gutter snipe of the press who hates me" praised the Secretary of State "for his wisdom."[102] He subsequently declined an appointment as First Secretary of the American Legation to St. Petersburg because the job did not pay enough (*L, 66*). Harte ridiculed his own campaign for a federal appointment in "The Office-Seeker," one of the squibs he wrote for the *New York Sun*. The narrator of this piece meets the Western bumpkin Expectant Dobbs in the lobby of a Washington hotel and by chance follows his sputtering attempts over the next several months to secure government employment. He had been promised a patronage job by the corrupt Gashwiler, who reneges on the pledge. Undeterred, Dobbs writes dozens of letters to such agencies as the Department of Tape and the Bureau for the Dissemination of Useless Information, until at length he becomes "quite seedy" in appearance, with "great hollows" around his eyes and "a slight flush on his cheek-bones" (I, 253). He finally is given a job "replenishing the pitchers in the various offices" in a "certain great department" of the government (I, 258), although with the advent of Civil Service Reform he is summarily fired: "the weak, foolish, emaciated head of Expectant Dobbs went to the block" (I, 259). On the last page of this bittersweet satire, Dobbs resolves to ask "one who is very potent with kings and councilors" to "interest Himself in my behalf" (I, 260), whereupon he lies back in bed and dies.

Like Expectant Dobbs, Harte enlisted the cooperation of the most influential men he knew—John Hay, Stanley Matthews, Carl Schurz, and others—in his bid for a diplomatic post. "As regards Appointments, I know nothing," he had reported to Anna in July 1877. "Whatever is done now, must come to me without solicitation" (Booth 1944, 136). Howells, who had written a campaign biography of Rutherford B. Hayes and whose wife Elinor was distantly related to the president, was persuaded to intervene on his behalf the following April. "I should be glad of his appointment, and I should have great hopes of him—and fears," he informed Hayes privately. "I have a great affection for the man," and "he has learned a terrible lesson in falling from the highest prosperity to the lowest adversity in literature" (*LLWDH* I, 251–52). This letter apparently turned the tide in Harte's favor. He was offered the post of Commercial Agent in Crefeld, Germany, in the Rhine valley near Düsseldorf. When he was shown the place on a map, he was told there was "not much to do" in the job, although he would be paid more than $2,000 annually to do it, and he leaped at the chance. He wrote Anna the next day that, "with all my disappointments, this seemed like a glimpse of Paradise" (*L*, 66). (When he got wind of the news, Twain vilified Harte in a letter to Howells as "a liar, a thief, a swindler, a snob, a sot, a sponge, a coward, a Jeremy Diddler. . . . Tell me what German town he is to filthify with his presence," he demanded from his hotel in Heidelberg, and "I will write the authorities there" [*MT–HL* I, 235–36].) Like the forty-niners who left their families in the States to prospect for gold, Harte sailed for Europe on 28 June 1878, leaving kith and kin in New Jersey ostensibly for reasons of economy. Whatever his intentions at the time, he would never return to the American shore.

Chapter Four

Consul and Man of Letters

Commercial Agent in Crefeld

No longer dependent upon the income from hackwork, Harte was able to put his literary career back on track, if only a narrow-gauge one, during his two-year stint as consul in Crefeld. Even before he arrived in Germany, he was well-known there. By 1873, he had attracted "more translators in Germany than he [could] number on his fingers."[1] The Berlin correspondent of the *Literary World* had reported in June 1877 that Germans considered Harte the "greatest" living American writer.[2] A German critic, T. T. Honegger, was almost as enthusiastic in the *Blätter für literarische Unterhaltung* in November 1877: "Bret Harte—ein amerikanischer Name! In kurzer Zeit hat sich dieser Mann einen gefeierten Ruf als Erzähler und Sittenzeichner erworben."[3] ("Bret Harte—an American name! In a short time, this man has gained a celebrated reputation as a storyteller and critic of morals.") According to Eugene Timpe, Harte's "Goldgräber Geschichten" were published in German translation more often during the 1870s than the works of any other American. Within 12 years of his introduction to German readers, he "had become the most popular American author" in the country, with more than 40 German editions of his works in print.[4] Indeed, Harte was "never more keenly and humanly touched," as he later remarked, than on the day after his arrival in the country. "I was wandering down the Konigsallee of Dusseldorf, in the utter loneliness and friendlessness of a foreigner to its language and people, when I caught sight of my own name, in German text, on certain little quaint-looking books, with queer titles, in a bookseller's window. It was like the hail of a friendly voice, and as I passed on, it seemed to me that I was no longer a stranger" (Rosenthal, 85). Harte related a similar story in a letter to Osgood: "I went into a bookstore here where English is alleged to be spoken. After I had made my purchase . . . I noticed a German translation of one of my books lying on the counter. Thinking to ingratiate myself with my new fellow citizens I picked up the book and with a modest smile, printed my name in large letters on the cover and said 'That is mine.' *Der Buchhandler* without a smile, took the book quietly but firmly from my hand, said 'das is fur my brudder in Stuttgart,' and turned scornfully away."[5] A few months later, in any event, Harte would write his friend John Hay, the U.S. Assistant Secretary of State, that before coming to Germany he had not had "the least idea of my tremendous popularity as a writer here. My books are everywhere" (M&M, 88).

He was not, in truth, a very efficient subconsul. Within two weeks of his arrival in Crefeld, he left for London "without leave from the Department. I shall at once apologize (when I return to my post) averring my ignorance as a novice" in the diplomatic service.[6] He later referred derisively to his "lofty and self-sacrificing devotion to the interests of my Government, which kept me here at the Consulate certifying to invoices,"[7] lubricating the commerce between his country and the region around Crefeld, well-known in the nineteenth century for the manufacture and export of silks and velvets. Harte delegated most of the paperwork in the job to his vice-consul, Rudolf Schneider, especially after his first reports were criticized for their "poetic numbers and figures of rhetoric."[8] As a result, of course, he had more time to write.

He still needed the money he earned from his pen, albeit not quite so desperately as before. He sent his wife his entire consular salary and lived on the income from his literary work and occasional lectures. Twain would later allege that Harte had "deserted his family," that he "never sent them a dollar" and "never intended to send them a dollar" while abroad (*MTE*, 291). Harte, however, did mail his wife regular monthly checks totaling about $60,000 over the next 24 years.[9] As long as he held a salaried position in the government, moreover, he was chased by bill collectors. He was hardly settled in Crefeld before he received a bill from the Stuyvesant House in New York dated 1874 for an outstanding balance of $300. "I was completely *stunned*," he wrote Anna. "It is of course quite improbable that any such bill can be legally collected here, the lawyers say, and at all events I have nothing they can take from me. . . . I did not think it possible that I had any creditor so contemptible."[10] Before leaving the United States Harte also promised "to pay up my indebtedness to Dana" by writing a few pieces for the *New York Sun* (*L*, 111). Within a month of his transatlantic crossing, he completed the manuscript of his first European sketch, "A Tourist from Injianny," the comic account of a rustic Hoosier and his daughter on a grand tour. "We saw Switzerland and Italy, and if I hed n't been short o' time we'd hev gone to Egypt," the old man announces (XI, 350). Vaguely reminiscent of "Daisy Miller," which Harte thought "quite fresh and entertaining" but for its "almost absurdly illogical conclusion" (*L*, 158), the story ends with the daughter's marriage to an English nobleman rather than with her death—the type of adolescent wish-fulfillment common in fairy tales.

Although he was more than 6,000 miles from the mining country in northern California, Harte also continued to write what Bierce would call "Warmed–overland" stories with an economic subtext. In "An Heiress of Red Dog" (1878), for example, an eccentric miner bequeaths his entire estate—including 1,000 shares in the Rising Sun Mining Company worth $3 million—to Peggy Moffat, "a freckle-faced maid-servant" at a local hotel, on the singular condition that she "never share" her good fortune "with any man or woman" whom she loves (XXIV, 397, 419). When "the handsome, graceless vagabond" Jack Folinsbee (XXIV, 408) proposes marriage to her, she offers him a weekly allowance of only $25. The feckless Folinsbee tells her "to go to —— with her money," abandons his suit, and leaves Red Dog (XXIV, 411). This story, like "The Iliad of Sandy Bar," seems in retrospect nothing less than Harte's veiled comment on his ruptured relations with Mark Twain (whose sister Pamela was, significantly enough, surnamed Moffett). Peg's claim to the miner's wealth withstands challenges by his widow and others: in this way Harte acknowledges Twain's supremacy among all Western writers. Despite the appearance of "niggardliness and greed" (XXIV, 414), Peg loves the dissipated Folinsbee just as, Harte suggests, Twain had befriended him in the throes of his distress. Peg's offer of $25 a week was conditioned by her love for Folinsbee much as Twain had been willing to pay him $25 a week to collaborate with him on another play. This story may be read as Harte's expression of regret for the haste with which he had spurned Twain's offer. Unfortunately, the disguised public apology—if that is what it is—failed to repair the rift between the two men. Harte's English publishers sent Twain a copy of *An Heiress of Red Dog and Other Tales* when it appeared in the spring of 1879, presumably at Harte's request, and Twain read the volume at least twice (*MT–HL* I, 261). But his anger would not abate, and they would never meet again.

"Jeff Brigg's Love Story" (1880) was more of the same "old gruel,"[11] a tale which illustrates the "striking contrast" between a rustic Westerner and his genteel Eastern love interest (Quinn, 237). Jefferson Briggs, the proprietor and landlord of the halfway house at the Summit, rescues a beautiful young invalid and "modest virgin" (XX, 372), the daughter of Eastern tourists, from a stagecoach half submerged by flood waters. Basking in the California sun, she soon recovers her health. "This mountain air has been like balm to me," she declares. "I feel I am growing stronger day by day" (XX, 339). Predictably, Jeff and Jessie fall in love, but not without the inevitable complications: Jeff goes broke and loses the title to his hotel. The young couple drift apart and Jeff begins to drink and gamble. After he saves Yuba Bill from an attack of road agents, however, he again crosses paths with Jessie and they marry. "The name of Briggs remained a power in Tuolumne and Calaveras County," Harte concludes by way of benediction (XX, 431). At least one reviewer dismissed the story as "a mushy mess of improbable nonsense."[12]

During his residence in Germany, Harte also wrote several stories and two or three poems with a distinctly Teutonic flavor. He attempted to adapt his interest in local color, particularly in local dialect and customs, to the German scene. The experiment was not entirely a success, however. The poems are utterly forgettable, written for quick sale to magazines. At nearly 300 lines, "A Legend of Cologne" is "a good honest length," Harte wrote his agent, and it "ought to be worth about" $125 (*L*, 119). The hackneyed couplets of "The Legends of the Rhine" seem little more than a rhyming exercise in iambic tetrameter:

> Maledictions, whispered vows
> Underneath the linden boughs;
> Murder, bigamy, and theft;
> Travelers of goods bereft;
> Rapine, pillage, arson, spoil,—
> Everything but honest toil,
> Are the deeds that best define
> Every Legend of the Rhine. (VIII, 307)

Whenever Harte tried to "deal with life in other regions" than California, as the *Athenaeum* concluded in 1879, his work was "commonplace."[13]

As a political appointee, he had, after all, picked his assignment almost literally from a map. Although he was not a native Californian, he had at least been intimately familiar with the habits of those who lived in the West. He spoke the idiom of the people in both Spanish and English. But in Germany Harte was ever the alien who knew little of the language before he arrived and scarcely knew more of it when he left. "I am doing very little" in Crefeld, he admitted to Hay in December, except to "wrestle with the language and wait for a verb to come round the corner and help me" (M&M, 85). "Papa has begun to study German like a child," he wrote his young son the next month, "and has been in the third and fourth reader, and has broken his heart and worn his eyes out" (L, 124). Harte apparently acquired only the most rudimentary understanding of German and Germany during his two years in the country. He behaved, in fact, rather like a boor, disparaging in his private letters not only the "horrid" language, but the "damnable" cuisine, the "miserable" hotels, the "grim, black, bitter" climate, the "distasteful" festivals, even the "diabolically ludicrous and stupidly monotonous" opera (L, 142, 85, 115, 81, 128). He attended a performance of *Tannhäuser* in January 1879, for example, and reported to his wife that "In the third act, I think, Tannhäuser and two other minstrels sang before the King and Court to the accompaniment of their harps—and the boiler factory. Each minstrel sang or rather declaimed something like the multiplication table for about 20 minutes" (L, 129). He was impressed by some of the "wonderfully" uniformed soldiers he saw on the streets, though he quickly tired of military "glitter." "Every other man you meet in Düsseldorf, Coblenz, and Mayence is a soldier," he complained (L, 126).

For most of Harte's tenure in Germany, he did not even live in Crefeld but in Düsseldorf, in part because he felt snubbed by the Crefeld town authorities. As he complained to Hay in February 1880, "during my 18 months residence here I have not received the *first* official civility or even recognition from Mayor or Burgomaster. My cards have been unacknowledged" (M&M, 88). He thought the town "the most uninteresting place you ever saw" and compared it to "a cramped Philadelphia without its neatness" or "Paterson, New Jersey, without its contiguity to a great city" (L, 86; M&M, 88). In Düsseldorf, at least, he became fast friends with General von Rauch, the local military commander, and he was "in society." In May 1879, he attended a formal dinner hosted by the Provincial Diet, "a long tedious affair," as he wrote his wife, with "much wine-drinking, sentimental speech-making, etc." (L, 141). Predictably, all of Harte's stories with a German setting would be devoted to the international theme and would explore the juxtaposition of cultures from the point of view of the American abroad, rather like Washington Irving's *Tales of a Traveller,* although they are usually flawed by his veiled condescension to things German.

Still, parts of them are "charming," as Arthur Hobson Quinn has noted, and as a body of work they "would have added greatly to the reputation" of many lesser writers (Quinn, 240).

German Stories

Harte's provincialism is most evident in the first of his tales set in Germany, "A Legend of Sammtstadt," originally published in December 1878 in the *New York Sun*. Its provenance in the pages of the newspaper is relevant here: Harte pitched the story to an American audience. In its bare outlines, moreover, it is vaguely autobiographical. Sammtstadt or "Velvettown" is Harte's version of Crefeld, and the dyspeptic protagonist, James Clinch, is a caricature of the author. Clinch is a pompous philistine, an "innocent abroad," a prototype of the gauche American. He thinks that Germany, with its slow pace and decaying buildings, is "played out"—the phrase is a Western figure of speech that refers to the exhaustion of gold and silver mines—and he travels strictly by the guidebook because "he was too good an American to waste time in looking up uncatalogued curiosities" (XXV, 478). In the course of the story, Clinch falls asleep after sipping a glass of vintage wine and, like Rip Van Winkle, is transported in time, in this case back a century or two. When he awakens, he is a resplendent cavalier, nephew to one Baron Kölnsche of Köln and, as it turns out, the original immigrant to the quarter of Philadelphia known as Crefeld. When the past comes alive for him, Clinch becomes more liberal and tolerant of other cultures. Or as Ward Lewis explains, "The reader observes Clinch in the process of gradually acquiring knowledge and understanding beyond his national experience, of becoming more cosmopolitan."[14] Yet Harte spoils the effect of his epiphany by debunking the romantic legends of the Rhine elsewhere in the story. The dragon of the Drachenfels, Clinch learns, was in fact a "boar transformed by the drunken brains of the *Bauers*," and the legend of Lorelei originated when a young fellow "disappeared with the gamekeeper's daughter at Obercassel" (XXV, 500, 502). While the tale overtly satirizes chauvinism of the sort Harte expressed in his private letters, it subtly betrays this very same chauvinism by ridiculing Germans as sots and sinners. Twain objected to the air of "snobbishness" about the story, to Harte's affections and careless misspellings of German words, to "his jejune anxiety to display" his "laboriously acquired ignorance. . . . He rings in *Strasse* when street would answer every purpose, and *Bahnhof* when it carries no sharper significance to the reader than 'station' would" (*MT–HL* I, 261). Not surprisingly, the story would offend German readers for similar reasons.

When Bayard Taylor, the American ambassador to Germany, unexpectedly died in late December 1878, the editor of the *Berliner Tageblatt* asked Harte to supply an obituary for their paper, an assignment he handled so deftly[15] he was invited to write a series of articles giving his "frank, honest" impressions "of German Life and Character."[16] He apparently contributed, in the end, only one such sketch to the paper—"A Legend of Sammtstadt," recycled from the *New York Sun.* The "people of Crefeld were very much annoyed" by the piece, he reported to his wife, and took "the extravagant speeches I put in C[linch]'s mouth as my own utterance." Characteristically, he claimed the affair was all a misunderstanding and blamed it on the Germans with their "thin-skin" and "ridiculous sensitiveness." However, he decided to discontinue his series of articles. As he explained, "Writing them for a German paper and living in a German community, and above all holding a half-diplomatic position here, cramps my pen" (*L,* 139).

Harte prepared, it seems, at least one other sketch for the *Tageblatt,* although it did not appear there—a rumination entitled "Views from a German Spion" (1879). Just as "A Legend of Sammtstadt" borrowed its twist of plot from Irving's "Rip Van Winkle," this piece was apparently inspired by Hawthorne's "Sights from a Steeple." It is precisely the type of familiar essay Harte had agreed to contribute to the paper—a collection of random observations and impressions on a variety of topics from the point of view of "an American stranger" (XXIV, 509). It is quite literally a series of reflections, for Harte describes what he sees in the mirrors attached to his window casement "with a certain unobtrusiveness of angle that enables them to reflect the people who pass" (XXIV, 508). Noting "that a majority of those who pass my mirror have weak eyes" and wear glasses (XXIV, 509), for example, he speculates that the "abominable" German Fraktur script has caused almost universal eyestrain in the country. On his part, he admits, he must still grope his way "through a blind alley of substantives and adjectives, only to find the verb of action in an obscure corner" of the sentence (XXIV, 511)—giving a humorous turn in print to his private complaints about the awful German language. Overall, Harte's comments in this essay are reasonably good-natured and evenhanded, presumably because he wrote it for both American and German readers. Only near its close does he assume a patronizing tone.

Harte describes *Fasching* as an "annual celebration of the lower classes" and expresses near-pity for the "poor people" who must purchase a holiday under such "hard conditions" (XXIV, 522). "There was something almost pathetic to me," he writes, in their attempt to "mock the dreariness of their poverty" (XXIV, 525, 526). At one extreme, this essay was considered "a delightfully written chronicle of a hour spent in a German window-seat," and at the other as "a somewhat common-place magazine article."[17]

"Peter Schroeder" (1879), the only other story with a German setting Harte wrote while in Crefeld, is both his best and least finished story about Germany. Schroeder, or "Dutch Pete" as he is known to the mining camp of Spanish Gulch, is a '48er, a German who, after the failed Revolution of 1848, emigrated to America and struck it rich. A political idealist committed to free institutions and Republican principles, he sold his claim, enlisted in the Union army during the American Civil War, "and served until the Richmond surrender" (XXV, 329). Fifteen years later, back in Germany, he has settled into a dull routine. Compared to his experiences in the mining camps and on the battlefields of America, his life in retirement seems monotonous indeed, an unbroken chain of days that are "all alike—uniform, theatrical, and unreal" (XXV, 333). One day he is awakened from his nap by a party of Americans, all of them "pretty," "graceful," and "exceedingly well-dressed" (XXV, 335), whose "republican simplicity and social freedom" he "admired in theory" though "he was conscious that his new life had brought with it responsibilities to other customs" (XXV, 342–43). His visitors mock his allegiance to America when he shows them a small room he has decorated with the Stars and Stripes, a portrait of Abraham Lincoln, and his Union army uniform. When Schroeder allows that he received the Iron Cross for service in the Franco-Prussian War, one of them snorts, "*Iron* Cross! Couldn't afford a gold one, eh?" (XXV, 341). Ignorant of history and too-easily impressed by military pomp, these silly tourists are "headin' up the Rhine to tackle some of them ruined castles" (XXV, 342). Schroeder then states explicitly the apparent moral of the story: "Der rebooplicans don't got no memories. Ve don't got nodings else" (XXV, 344).

Would but the tale have ended here. Instead, it takes, as one reviewer remarked, a "too consciously pathetic" turn.[18] In effect, Harte begins an altogether new story at this point. What had been a study in differences between traditions and generations—to the advantage to the stolid German—suddenly becomes a study in imperialism. Schroeder is seduced by the promises of a wily political opportunist from California who plays upon his dreams of a just republic. "You are the stuff from which liberators and deliverers are made," this suntanned Mephistopheles insists. "What if I told you of another country, Peter,—newer and fresher than the one you once adopted; where the soil is virgin and the people are plastic,—a country to be moulded and fashioned into shape by men like you; a country with no predilections, few traditions, and *no* history; a republic wanting only ideas, and capital; a country that you might become president of . . . ?" (XXV, 352–53). Harte invokes the example here of William Walker, the American filibuster who conquered Nicaragua in 1856 and died before a firing squad in Honduras in 1860. For reasons that are vague at best, Schroeder bankrolls an expedition to colonize the fictional Latin American nation of Ometepe and, like Walker, is executed by a firing squad when the revolution fails. Harte has again undermined an otherwise favorable portrayal of a German, in this case with the gratuitous conclusion to the story. Overall, as the *Hartford Courant* opined, Harte's "German sketches are merely good magazine papers."[19]

Within a year of his arrival in Crefeld he was convinced that the weather there was "injurious to [his] temperament and condition" (*L,* 144), and his German physician soon confirmed his diagnosis: "the Doctor . . . cheerfully tells me that the climate is killing me here."[20] He repeatedly complained in his letters of a variety of respiratory and intestinal ailments, though a Berlin paper reported he was actually attempting to recover from a bout with alcoholism—a charge which apparently had some basis in fact, although it was quickly retracted when Harte threatened legal action.[21] "Physically I'm a little better I think,—morally I know I'm not," as he wrote a member of his family in September 1878.[22] he convinced the State Department to transfer him to Glasgow in the summer of 1880. However, he did not sever all ties with Germany. He befriended Herbert von Bismarck, son of the German chancellor, in 1885, for example, and he continued to correspond with Rudolf Schneider and his wife to the end of his life. He wrote them in August 1880 that he missed "our old gossiping chats, and the sympathy that was always ready for me when I used to come over growling and dyspeptic from Düsseldorf in the morning. I've been spoiled. I have become sentimental and *German*!! Think of it—what an awful retribution!"[24]

Long after Harte left Germany, his work remained popular there. Nearly all of his stories were translated into German and published in

such magazines as the *Deutsche Revue* and the *Deutsche Rundschau*.[25] On
the strength of his European popularity, in fact, he was invited to reply
to the "Toast to Literature" at the annual meeting of the Royal Academy in London on 1 May 1880, an "exceptional honor" he hoped
would "remind some of my countrymen that they might have been
civil when I went away."[26] Berthold Auerbach declared in the early
1880s that, while "Harte has never been American Minister at Berlin,"
he "is more popular there and throughout Germany than twenty Min-
isters," and Lewis Rosenthal wrote in 1885 that "Bret Harte is of all
living Americans the best known and most read in the Fatherland"
(Rosenthal, 85). "[M]y German readers are still loyal to me," he wrote
Frau Schneider in 1887, "and they do not appear to be yet tired of
translations of all I do."[27] He reported in 1893 that his work still
enjoyed its "greatest sale" among Germans (Haskell, 17).

Partly to appeal to this class of readers, he wrote two stories set in
Germany after visiting Cologne in the fall of 1895. He "made some
trips up and down the Rhine" and "basked in the sun, and the *sauer-
kraut,* and the dear old smell of pipes and dregs of beer glasses, which
reminded me of the old days" (*L,* 410–11). His final stories about
Germany are colored by these pleasant memories of the Rhineland.
"The Indiscretion of Elsbeth" (1895) is a diverting if trivial little tale
about a wry American journalist named Hoffmann who visits the village of his ancestors and quite by chance meets and falls in love with
a princess, the daughter of the local Grand Duke. (At least two copies
of the manuscript of this story are extant—in the Bancroft Library at
the University of California at Berkeley and the Alderman Library at
the University of Virginia—which raises the possibility that Harte not
only sold the text of the story to magazines but may have sold multiple
copies of the manuscript to collectors.) In "Unser Karl" (1897), Harte
gently burlesqued international diplomacy. The protagonist of this tale
is American consul in "the pretty linden-haunted German town" of
Schlachtstadt (XIII, 2), a bucolic version of Crefeld named for the soldiers garrisoned there. Harte had, it seems, revised his harsh impressions of the city over the years. Schlachtstadt is, like Crefeld, "known
all over the world for the manufactures of certain beautiful textile fab-
rics," and Consul Donnerwetter, like Harte during his service in the
diplomatic corps, is mostly responsible for "the examination and cer-
tification of divers invoices sent to his office" (XIII, 5). Occasionally,
however, he is asked to intervene in cases in which German immigrants
who become naturalized American citizens are arrested as military de-

serters when they return to visit their relatives. "In this way," Harte explains, "the consul had saved to Milwaukee a worthy but imprudent brewer, and to New York an excellent sausage butcher and possible alderman" and "thus the temper and peace of two great nations were preserved" (XIII, 8). The consul is fêted at a dinner, a comic account of the one Harte had attended in Düsseldorf in 1879 as the guest of the provincial parliament. After "the emptying of many bottles," the consul's health is toasted "in a neat address of many syllables containing all the parts of speech and a single verb," to which the consul, "tremulous with emotion and a reserve verb in his pocket," replies with a "generous panegyric" of his own (XIII, 20–21).

He declines to interfere, however, in the case of one Karl Schwartz, an innocent-looking cherub "scarcely out of his teens" (XIII, 9), who has a limp alibi and no immigration papers. "Our Karl" is pressed into service as a German military page and quickly rises through the ranks until he is the attaché to General Adlerkreutz, the local military commander (modeled upon Harte's old friend von Rauch). Schwartz is soon transferred "through some high official manipulation" to the governor's staff in the nearby city of Rheinfestung (read, Düsseldorf), "the key of the Rhine, the citadel of Westphalia" (XIII, 27), and then he disappears, apparently drowned by accident in the river. His body is never recovered. A few months later, en route to a new consular post, Donnerwetter meets him by chance in a Paris café. "Schwartz" is, it turns out, a captain in the French bureau of military intelligence, a native of Alsace, a spy who impersonated a German in order to infiltrate the German army and spy on the fortress at Rheinfestung. The consul had unwittingly cooperated in his scheme by failing to intervene on his behalf when he was first arrested. The story is, on the whole, the most satisfactory of all Harte's works about Germany. It is carefully plotted and, unlike his earlier pieces, betrays no hint of condescension toward its subject.

None of these pieces ranks with Harte's best work, to be sure, but in them may be traced his maturing appreciation for Germany and, if only indirectly, the revival of his literary career. As late as 1912, a decade after his death, Harte's books had appeared in more German editions than had Twain's, and in 1914 they were still considered bestsellers.[28] Even today, at least four German editions of his fiction are in print. His career did not end with his so-called exile from America in 1878; in fact, from all indications Germany was more hospitable to him than New York and Boston had been.

Consul in Glasgow

As was his wont, Harte disliked each city where he lived more than
the last one. In late July 1880, only four days after beginning his new
job in Scotland, he was in Paris to catch "one ray of blessed sunshine"
after three solid weeks of rain in Britain (*L,* 185). He wrote Anna
barely four months later that Glasgow "is a hundred times worse than
Crefeld—more *depressing,* and poisonous from chemical fumes from the
factories" (*L,* 191). He later complained that he felt as though he was
"living by gaslight in a damp cellar with an occasional whiff from a
drain, from a coal-heap, from a mouldy potato-bin, and from dirty
washtubs" (*L,* 214–15). Although his annual consular salary increased
to $3,000, and "other emoluments . . . ma[d]e it at least" $4,000 (*L,*
173), his leaves of absence, whether authorized or not, seem to have
doubled. As in Crefeld, Harte entrusted much of his work to his vice-
consul, in this case "a hard-headed Scotch lawyer" named William
Gibson (*L,* 205). During his five years in Glasgow, in fact, he sent
Gibson no fewer than 562 letters and telegrams, a number that "makes
certain that he must have been away" from the office "an extraordinary
large proportion of his time" (Stewart, 271). The novelist William
Black compared him to a "globule of mercury" or a "wandering comet.
The only place he is sure not to be found in is at the Glasgow Consu-
late."[29] Harte exploited the proximity of his new post to London,
where he moved in the same social circles as Trollope, Hardy, Henry
James, George Eliot, and the historian James Froude. He sometimes
crossed paths with James Russell Lowell, the American Minister to the
Court of St. James, although "they did not meet often or willingly.
Lowell owned the brilliancy and uncommonness of Harte's gift," as
Howells recalled, but "surfeited his passion of finding everybody more
or less a Jew by finding that Harte was at least half a Jew on his father's
side."[30] Harte was especially intimate with Arthur Van de Velde, a
Belgian diplomat, and his wife Marguerite, in whose home he usually
stayed during his visits to London. "I have a room there always known
as mine," he explained to Anna, and the Van de Veldes "adopted me
into their family—Heaven knows how or why—as simply as if I had
known them for years" (*L,* 215). Although Harte attributed the talk
about his "alleged absences" from Glasgow to the "hundreds hungry
for my place" in the diplomatic corps, and though he professed to be
"*rather* a good Consul" (*L,* 194, 208, 205, 235), his dereliction of duty
did not go entirely unnoticed. James G. Blaine later remarked that

Harte irreparably damaged his reputation in official circles by becoming "the worst consul thus far recorded" (M&M, 78).

Despite his larger government salary, which he simply forwarded to his family in America, Harte continued to hatch new schemes to supplement his income. He was approached in the summer of 1880 by several "English Capitalists" who offered "to start me in a magazine of my own in London" to be called *Bret Harte's Monthly* (M&M, 93). "It will enable me to control my own publications and really profit by my own stories," he hoped, and it "would enable me to turn my editorial faculty to account" (*L,* 184). Like *The Capital,* however, this ill-fated venture collapsed before a single issue could be published amid rumors that *Harper's Monthly* was about to appear in an English edition. Harte also proved his loyalty to his political superiors in Washington by writing the introduction to F. H. Mason's biography of James Garfield, the new president, and he delivered his lecture "The Argonauts of '49" on whistle-stop tours throughout England. Lewis Carroll heard him speak in April 1880 and referred in his diary to the "quiet humour" of the address.[31] Harte wrote Frau Schneider in December that he had "lectured three times in the last three days, on the smallest possible amount of strength, and purely by nerve force."[32] Given the competing demands on his time and the temporary loss of his "old desire for work" (*L,* 204), Harte completed no new fiction between mid–1880 and early 1882. He returned to his writing desk shortly after the death of Longfellow in March 1882 to eulogize "the man I most revered" in a piece for *Good Words.* He recalled with emotion how the poet had welcomed him to Craigie House in Cambridge while he was yet in the first flush of his fame only 12 years before (Kozlay, 250). The stories Harte wrote after the hiatus also had a more hard-bitten and cynical edge to them. In "Found at Blazing Star" (1882), for example, the heroine discovers the body of a murdered man with a "bluish hole above the right temple" and a hand "across the swollen abdomen" (XXIII, 386–87). The *Literary World* lambasted the author for depicting scenes "so crude and offensive as to be in melancholy contrast" to his "previous treatment of similar materials."[33] Harte privately acknowledged the force of such criticism. "I wish I was more cheerful," he wrote at the time, "but my stories lately seem all very sad. I'm getting old I suppose."[34]

These disturbed and disquieting tales, often punctuated with a sexual prurience that Henry Adams noted in his *Education,*[35] are epitomized by "Flip: A California Romance" (1882). The teenaged Flip Fairley, a "freckled Diana of the spicy wilderness"[36] with "tawny" hair, "shapely limb," "tanned bare arms," and a "lithe, nymph-like figure" (XXIII, 302–304, 324), falls in love with the handsome desperado Lance (!) Harriott. To his "excited fancy" she seems "to personify the perfume and intoxication of her native woods," and their first kiss "thrill[s] him" with "a subtle fire" (XXIII, 323, 324). Much as Flip teases Lance, moreover, Harte titillates the reader with a peek of Flip at her bath in the forest, a risqué passage at least one modern reader has described with the phrase "soft-core":[37]

Satisfied that no intruding foot had invaded that virgin bower, she returned to her bath and began to undress. A slight wind followed her, and seemed to whisper to the circumjacent trees. It appeared to waken her sister naiads and nymphs, who, joining their leafy fingers, softly drew around her a gently moving band of trembling lights and shadows, of flecked sprays and inextricably mingled branches, and involved her in a chaste sylvan obscurity, veiled alike from pursuing god or stumbling shepherd. Within these hallowed precincts was the musical ripple of laughter and falling water, and at times the glimpse of a lithe brier-caught limb, or a ray of sunshine trembling over bright flanks, or the white austere outline of a childish bosom. (XXIII, 333–34)

Harte endows Flip with a "mysterious instinct of maturing womanhood" (XXIII, 344), a precocious sexuality she apparently inherited from her maniacal father. Old David Fairley labors under the peculiar delusion that he can make diamonds from charcoal. A widower, he spends his days heaving pine logs into a pit fire, a symbolic act of copulation. The children of such a varmint are likely to be promiscuous and depraved, Harte implies, and so in the last chapter he kills off Flip and her lover in a grisly murder–suicide.

If in such tales as "Jeff Briggs's Love Story" he erred on the side of sentimentality, in those like "Flip" and "In the Carquinez Woods" (1883) Harte overcompensated for the mistake in the direction of lurid sensationalism. In the latter story, a noble mixed-blood named Low Dorman (or L'Eau Dormante) is figuratively torn between two young women: the fair Nellie Wynn, daughter of the pastor of the local First Baptist Church, and the dark lady Teresa, former dancer at the Alhambra saloon. Once again, however, these characters play against type: Nellie is, despite the appearance of sophistication and virtue, a fool and a coquette. She is "profoundly ignorant in two languages, with a trained misunderstanding of music and painting" (II, 383), and she yields to the temptation of forbidden love by sneaking into the woods for clandestine trysts with the "half-breed" Low. Alone with him, she audaciously removes her shoes and stockings and dangles her toes in a natural spring, flaunting "her little feet shining through the dark water" (II, 300). In the sexual shorthand of the period, Miss Nellie has gone skinny-dipping. On her part, the *mestiza* Teresa reforms while hiding out from the law in Low's forest sanctuary. "I've made myself out worse than I was," she tells her protector (II, 280), whose socks she soon begins to darn. Teresa's profane lover Dick Curson (read, cursin'), whom she is accused of killing, happens not to have died after all; that is, she repents for a crime that it turns out she did not commit. She falls in love with Low, of course, and yearns for a chance to prove to him "that a brunette and a woman of her experience was better than an immature blonde" such as Miss Nellie (II, 329). By a badly managed quirk of fate, the sheriff trailing Teresa happens to be Low's father by a Cherokee squaw. As the *Spectator* groused, Harte "does not take the pains" in this story "to finish off any of his characters very carefully; nor, indeed, are they, for the most part, worth the trouble"; and the *Dial* dismissed the tale as "a dismal legend of gnomes and demons and furies."[38] Although the text explicitly commends racial toleration, Harte in its last pages recoils in apparent horror at the implicit logic of the story, at his own defense of miscegenation, as if he was surprised to discover what "In the Carquinez Woods" was about even as he was writing it. Sometimes he lost control of his stories, as he once admitted: "The fact is my characters *will not* do as they ought to do" (*L,* 347). In the end, he neither approves nor acquiesces to race-mixing but wipes the slate clean: the "half-breed" who kissed a white woman in the woods, the half-white woman who loved him, and the father who sired him all perish in a fire that rages through the Carquinez Woods.

These stories with their gruesome endings were, predictably, among the least popular of Harte's mature works, although he soon reverted to form. He knocked out a so-called pot-boiler entitled "At the Mission of San Carmel" for Christmas 1882 (*L,* 214), and he followed his tired and tested formula to the letter in "Left Out on Lone Star Mountain," the yarn he spun for Christmas 1883. Harte sold the latter story to the *New York Sun* on the basis of a plot synopsis he sent Dana: it

briefly chronicles how four partners—a deliciously irresistable quartette of idle Bohemians—finally resolve to change their failures by giving up their utterly "played out" but only half-worked claim at "Lone Star" to their fifth partner, who in spite of his years and boyish half-poetic tastes, has been a kind of guardian to them, takes it to heart . . . , imagines revenges, etc., but discovering on the day they leave that a land slide on the claim—now *his*—has revealed an auriferous deposit, he relents and seeks them. Meanwhile, they become remorseful and disgusted and seek *him,* coming together in time to find that *another slide* has taken place completely burying the desired vein. Of course they come to the conclusion the gold *is there still,* accept the obvious lesson, and are reconciled as the coach, which should have borne them away, dashes by, the jovial expressman's greeting revealing a fact that in their utter isolation, and the peculiar quality of the California Season, they had forgotten—that it was indeed "Merry Christmas"!

The story may be negatively described as having no trace or hint of a petticoat in it. The feminine gender does not appear from first to last. And except in the last line the word "Christmas" does not occur.[39]

This agrarian idyl, untroubled by "petticoats" and other pests and with its precious smirks at the reader, is virtually a parody of Harte's best work. Little wonder that J. A. Noble derided the author in the *Academy* at the time as a "man of real genius who has largely given himself over to the production of pot-boilers."[40]

The cheesy quality of these stories was, obviously, related to his renewed compulsion in 1883–84 to make as much money as quickly as possible. He was still "harried by old bills," hounded by creditors in America who "demanded their pound of flesh."[41] He was sued in the summer of 1883 for payment of an old tailor's bill—he would not pay the $230 in damages and costs until September 1886[42]—fueling the fear he would face a hoard of such suits should he return to America even for a visit. Though he was granted a three-month leave of absence by the State Department in late 1883, he remained in Britain. "You know that, although I have been keeping free from any new debts while I have been abroad," he wrote Anna from Glasgow in August, "there are old ones unpaid in America—and in some cases *judgements* have been procured. My creditors have not abated a single jot of their claims; nothing but a certain immunity I hold by being *here* keeps me from being harried perpetually by them."[43] When she replied with protests and recriminations, he conceded her point without changing his plans: "I suppose I am 'a strange man'—but you must try to think Nan that I am trying to be a more practical one than I have ever been."[44] While their marriage was never formally dissolved, they would never live together again. He hinted at their irreconcilable dif-

ferences in one of his stories published during the early 1880s: "It takes
the legal matrimonial contract to properly develop the first-class tyrant" (XX, 335). Harte's return to the U.S. was planned, then postponed, year by year. Sometimes his excuses were extremely lame, as
when he claimed Garfield's assassination in the summer of 1881 "not
only stopped my visit to Washington but kept me in England,"[45] or
when he pleaded the inadvisability of leaving his post before an election
(L, 251). More typically, however, he deferred the trip on financial
grounds, either because he feared "the smallest and most doubtful and
forgotten bill in account against me will be actively [reissued] when I
return,"[46] or because he first needed to complete a lucrative literary
assignment that would make a tentative later visit "a *certainty*" (L, 308,
310). He refused even to consider resettling in the States for similar
reasons: "I remain in England because I have the best market there,
and because I am enabled to keep my copyright in both Europe and
America."[47]

Regardless how financially secure he seemed, he worried he would
lose his consular post as the result of a change of administrations in
Washington. "My affairs have prospered" since he arrived in Europe,
or so he waxed reflectively in September 1883; "I have a market for
my wares; I am not dependent upon publishers' whims or caprices; I
have had no extraordinary expenses; I have been kept in my official
position without any effort on my part and against outside influences."
Still, he feared the "one step" or "unconscious act" that would "change
the luck" (L, 237). The longer he was ensconced in Glasgow, paradox-
ically, the more tenuous and uncertain his appointment became. He
had discouraged Anna from moving to Glasgow as early as July 1880
on the grounds he was liable to lose his job there if Garfield was de-
feated in the fall campaign: "my position in the Government service is
sure only up to the 4th of next March" and were he "to leave the
Government service, I could not make enough money by mere literary
work in England to support my family" (L, 182). After the election,
he hoped Civil Service Reform would give him "enough security to
enable me to look forward a year or two at least" but, as he learned to
his dismay, the legislation did not cover presidential appointments
"like mine."[48] His letters in 1884–85 echo the same anxious refrain:
"the possibility of bettering my condition, or *retaining* it through another Administration" (L, 251). "I do not buoy myself up with any
hope or expectation but keep along at my literary and Consular work,"
he averred.[49]

After Grover Cleveland, the Democratic candidate, was elected president in November 1884, Harte vainly maneuvered to remain in office. "The new administration may remove or promote me," he reported three weeks after Cleveland's inauguration. Dana and Charles Watrous intervened on his behalf, and even Hay "went to Washington to see if he couldn't do something for me with the administration he despises."[50] "My friends in America are doing all they can to keep me here, and all write to me that the Government does not look upon my appointment here as a *political* one—like the others," he wrote Frau Schneider in late May 1885. "But I shall be surprised at nothing."[51] Much as Hawthorne had been fired from the Salem Custom House by a new administration in 1849, Harte was "decapitated" in July, albeit with one significant difference: in his case there was no public outcry. Because he was away in London during a surprise visit by a State Department auditor, Harte was ostensibly dismissed for "inattention to duty," a "gratuitous insult" he answered by conscientiously remaining at his post until his successor arrived in late August (*L, 284*). "I was not unprepared nor greatly disappointed" when the ax fell, he reminisced later, "what with the increase[d] army of office seekers to be provided for. I have been lucky to have been retained so long."[52]

"St. Kentigorn" Stories

Soon after leaving government service, Harte wrote a satirical ditty, a kind of open letter to the administration that had fired him, defending the conduct of his office while in Glasgow. In this poem, the former consul asserted that he had faithfully discharged his duties, however onerous or contemptible they may have been:

I'm acquainted with affliction, chiefly in the form of fiction, as it is
    offered up by strangers at the consul's open door;
And I know all kinds of sorrow that relief would try to borrow with
    various sums, from six-pence upward to a penny more;
And I think I know all fancy styles of active mendicancy, from the
    helpless Irish soldier who mixed in our country's war;
And who laid in Libby prison in a war that wasn't his'n, and I sent back
    to the country—that he never saw before.
I know the wretched seaman who was tortured by a demon Captain 'till
    he fled in terror with his wages in arrears;
And I've given him sufficient to ship as an efficient and active malefactor
    with a gentle privateer.

Oh, I know the wealthy tourist who (through accident the purest) lost
    his letters, watch, and wallet from the cold deck coming o'er;
And I heeded that preamble, and lent him enough to gamble till he won
    back all his money on "a cold deck" here ashore!

He had learned, as a diplomat, more than he ever wished to know
about schemes, scams, and "ethical confusion."[53] These experiences had
seemed, at the time, barren of material he might use in his literary
work.

A decade later, however, he published a series of four stories, collec-
tively a study in the permutations of class difference, which represent
his last serious attempt to break with the western formula he had
helped to invent. Inspired by the "Consular Experiences" chapter of
Hawthorne's *Our Old Home,* these comedies of manners share a common
character, an unnamed American consul in the Scottish city of St. Kentigorn (read, Glasgow), a genial, middle-aged observer and cosmopol-
ite obviously modeled upon the author. As in his German tales,
however, Harte labored at a disadvantage: he had little more than a
tourist's knowledge of local Scottish color and scenery. "Because I am
an American," he admitted later, he "could not depict English character truthfully" (Haskell, 17). He urged the illustrator, his friend
Alexander S. Boyd, to correct "any outrages in Scotch dialect or Scotch
customs that, as an ignorant foreigner," he may have included (*L,*
377). In "The Heir of the McHulishes" (1893), a "degenerate" American arrives in St. Kentigorn to claim the "title and property" of an
ancient Scottish family (XX, 160). Although he is a "crank" and "an
impossible sort of lunatic," he attracts the attention of a social-climb-
ing Southern belle interested in his patrimony until she learns she
"would acquire no title merely through her marriage" to him (XX,
184). The sham heir eventually buys some northern highlands in what
"had simply resolved itself into an ordinary business speculation" for
$100,000, "half cash and half in Texas and Kentucky grass lands,"
from Lord Duncaster—who is in fact "the direct and sole heir" of the
McHulishes (XX, 178, 214–15, 220). The status-hungry American
may buy a title and a landed estate, but he is duped in the bargain.
"The Desborough Connections" (1898) essentially inverts this plot. In
this tale, the consul assists a nouveau riche American family in a "genealogical inquiry" into their ancestral roots (XIII, 124). Young Sadie
Desborough locates her grandfather on the estate of an old English
countryhouse, Scrooby Priory (read, Castle Ashby, medieval home of
Harte's friend the Earl of Compton). He is not lord of the manor, but

a "gaunt, half-crazy, overworked peasant, content to rake the dead leaves before the rolling chariots of the Beverdales" (XIII, 159). A true republican by virtue of her American birth, Sadie declines the marriage proposal, which would have installed her as mistress of the Priory and social superior of her relatives on the estate and, later, she honors her grandfather's memory by erecting "a soaring shaft of pure marble" at his grave (XIII, 178).

Perhaps the best of the St. Kentigorn stories is "Young Robin Gray" (1894), in which the consul inadvertently acts the part of a matchmaker. Through his accidental agency, the American patrician Robert (or Robin) Gray woos and weds the wee Scottish lass Ailsa Callender despite the initial objections of her stubbornly independent father. "He's a decent enough lad, and not above instructin'," the elder Callender admits, but he is also "extraordinar' extravagant" (XIX, 111). Whereas in the first two stories class differences post almost insurmountable obstacles to marriage, here those same obstacles are miraculously overcome. Harte squared the circle in the fourth story in the series, "A Rose of Glenbogie" (1894), which incidentally taps the tradition of English ghost and mystery fiction. In this tale, which T. Edgar Pemberton called a "finely drawn cabinet picture of Scotch character" (Pemberton, 246), the consul is an unwitting witness to a vulgar sexual intrigue. During a visit to Glenbogie House (probably the Van de Veldes' summer house in Bournemouth), he hears bumps in the night which, as it turns out, are not supernatural in origin but merely the result of some discreet extramarital "woman-stalking" among the gentry (XIX, 210). That is, Harte subtly satirizes the not-so-genteel manners of the monied class, subverting the very notion of social superiority on which the other three stories in the series turn. In all, according to the *Athenaeum* in 1898, Harte's later stories "dealing with European topics deserve to become favorites" and appeal to "both English and American readers."[54] While the St. Kentigorn series pointed his career in a promising new direction, Harte was unfortunately compelled for financial reasons to satisfy editors' and readers' expectations for more tailings from the old claim. He was, in the 1890s as in the 1870s, the sort of writer the market made him.

Later Plays

Like Howells and Henry James, Harte tried repeatedly over the years to capitalize on his reputation by writing popular drama, albeit with mixed success. He harbored few illusions about the literary merit of these plays; rather, as he often admitted in his letters, they were scripted mainly to make money. Plays are "vastly more profitable" than fiction, he noted in 1882 (*L, 207*). A "good popular play," he explained to Anna in 1884, "ought to give me certainly $3,000 a year for a year or two" (*L, 252*). He echoed the point five years later: a play earning royalties "seems to me my only hope of getting some relief to this perpetual grinding out of literary copy which is exhausting me, and no doubt the public."[55] Thus between 1882 and 1897, Harte wrote his 11 plays (see accompanying table) with six different coauthors, all of them Europeans, for reasons more legal than literary: he wished to prevent his creditors in America from attaching receipts "that might arise from [any] play in America—by making it payable to my *collaborateur* here who is not an American."[58] (He also outlined at least two librettos between 1882 and 1902 based on his stories "At the Mission of San Carmel" and "The Strange Experience of Alkali Dick," though neither of these works was apparently completed.) All of these scripts were completed; however, only one was ever produced.

Date	Play	Source story	Collaborator
1. early 1882	*Thankful Blossom*	"Thankful Blossom"	Mme. Van de Velde
2. fall 1882–fall 1885	*The Luck of Roaring Camp*	"The Luck of Roaring Camp"	Mme. Van de Velde
3. mid-1883	*Germaine*	*Germaine*	Edmond About
4. mid-1884–early 1885	*A Frontier Penelope*	"A Blue Grass Penelope"	Mme. Van de Velde
5. early to mid-1886	*Furnished by Bunter*	?	John L. Toole
6. mid 1886–fall 1889	*Gabriel Conroy*	*Gabriel Conroy*	Unknown
7. winter 1889–May 1890	*M'liss*	"M'liss"	Joseph Hatton
8. late 1894–fall 1896	*Sue*	"The Judgment at Bolinas Plain"	T. E. Pemberton
9. fall 1896	*Clarence*	"Clarence"	T. E. Pemberton
10. mid-1897	*Rushbrook*	"A Maecenas of the Pacific Slope"	T. E. Pemberton

11. fall 1897   *Held Up*   "Snowbound at   T. E. Pemberton
                                  Eagle's"

Harte's collaborations with Mme. Van de Velde were particularly
limp: first they worked together on adapting "Thankful Blossom," a
"play wh[ich] Shakespeare ought to have written," as he wrote Augustin Daly (Felheim, 297). Obviously, Harte and Van de Velde were not
equal to the task. He recalled years later that "whatever there was of
flower to [the story] escaped in its new focus and the livid colors looked
tawdry."[57] Incredibly, Van de Velde translated the script into French
and Harte tried to peddle it to Parisian producers.[58] Next they turned
"The Luck of Roaring Camp" into a young lady who visits Paris with
a group of gold miners. The heroine, as Harte explained to Daly, is "a
kind of intelligent 'fille du Regiment,' a sort of boyish ingénue" surrounded by "all my old characters" (Daly, 362–63). He admittedly
neglected his consular duties "to work at my new Play" in Bournemouth.[59] Although he also acknowledged a certain "loss of the poetic
element" in the dramatization of the story, Harte read a draft of this
play aloud to Hay and Clarence King in October 1882 and announced
that it was "finished" after "many alterations" in February 1883.[60] But
theatrical managers in London thought it "something so *new* in idea"
that they were "more or less afraid to risk it with English actors and
English audiences."[61] Back in New York, Boucicault was "too doubtful
of the success of the piece" even to bid on it.[62] Meanwhile, Harte had
collaborated with Edmond About in an adaptation of About's novel
Germanie. Boucicault thought enough of this script to forward it to the
theatrical impresario Lester Wallach, but nothing would come of this
project, either. "It seems hard that I have three plays," two of them
"representing six months of hard work—lying idle,—as so much unemployed capital," Harte groused. "Of course I would rather have their
failures in *MS* than before the footlights" (*L,* 234). In August 1883,
Daniel Frohman finally offered to pay a royalty of $10 per performance
for *The Luck,* mostly for the rights to Harte's title and name: "He said
the play 'would require a great deal of overhauling and changing.'"
Harte insisted on both higher royalties and script approval. Frohman
finally agreed to mount the play at the Madison Square Theatre in New
York in the fall of 1884, then reconsidered and asked Harte to rewrite
it. "This is the play that I expected would be paying me a royalty this
autumn!" he complained in June 1884. "The work must be done at
once—it will take the better part of two months to complete." He

considered sending Frohman a new play, his adaptation of "A Blue
Grass Penelope," in lieu of a wholesale revision (*L*, 252). In all, Harte
tinkered with *The Luck* intermittently for some three years but, apart
from a small forfeiture fee paid by Frohman, he never received a cent
for it. Instead, in 1890, he sold Boucicault dramatic rights to the
name, characters, and incidents of his original story.[63]

Harte's collaborations with professional actors and playwrights between 1886 and 1890 were no more successful than his earlier adap-
tations. He repeatedly struck the same notes in his letters of the period.
As he reported in April 1886, "I have been asked to collaborate with
one or two good dramatic authors in a dramatization of my 'Gabriel
Conroy' for the stage. There is just now a great demand for fresh
plays." More than two years later, he confessed that "I have been having
great annoyance and greater disappointment with the dramatization of
'Gabriel Conroy,' which seems to be going the way of all my dramatic
ventures." The play still lingered "on the stocks" the next year. Still,
as Harte explained, "I am very anxious that it should not be a *fiasco*."[64]
He first described his work with Joseph Hatton on "M'liss" in July
1889: "In the last three weeks I have been engaged in another bit of
dramatizing with a collaborator who is in the profession. . . . It *looks*
more practical than my other ventures of the kind." He even sketched
the set and helped design costumes for the production. By May 1890,
however, he had concluded that the play "will go over to the autumn
[of 1890] before it sees the footlights for the first time." The London
manager who had earlier agreed to produce it insisted upon first stag-
ing Twain's *The Prince and the Pauper*. Harte eventually abandoned the
project because "the episodes of the *story* would not make episodes of a
play."[65] Finally, in the spring of 1890, having written seven plays in
the past eight years and receiving virtually nothing for his efforts,
Harte resigned the attempt to write for the stage.

But only temporarily. Five years later, Pemberton, an experienced
playwright whom Harte had known since 1879, proposed to dramatize
his story "The Judgment of Bolinas Plain." Harte again rose to the
bait. To write a successful play "is one of my old illusions," he conceded, "but it has now been put in a more positive shape than any
other offer I have had. However, I do not hope *much*, and shall not be
disappointed" (*L*, 398). Pemberton was the ideal collaborator—a trust-
worthy friend, a "non–American," a competent technician who seemed
to Harte "to understand the business thoroughly."[66] They worked together on the script of *Sue*, as they entitled the play, for six months—
Pemberton patiently drafting scenes and Harte suggesting changes and

revising dialogue. As he explained in a letter to Pemberton in May 1895, for example, "We *never! never! never!* in America say 'whiskey *plain*' but always 'whiskey *straight*' or '*straight* whiskey'—which I think you will admit is a little more forcible slang."[67] In contrast to his earlier collaborations, Harte seems never to have become discouraged or disenchanted with the plays he wrote with Pemberton—he readily confessed to his "preoccupation with 'Sue'" even as they were polishing the script.[68] In May 1896, Charles Frohman agreed to produce the melodrama and advanced each of the authors £25, the most money Harte had earned as a playwright in nearly 20 years. As he remarked, "It quite startled me to find 'Sue' actually *born* and alive to *that* extent!"[69] He assured his wife he had not "sold my rights in it" outright but expected "to receive a share of its profits as long as it keeps the stage." He gave Pemberton the credit for selling the script to Frohman, "who, I dare say, would not have looked at it in *my* hands" (*L,* 430). With Pemberton's help, *Sue* easily became the most successful of Harte's plays.

Nevertheless, it was, as Howells protested, "almost as bad in structure and false in motive as a play could very well be." That is, Howells believed, it was ripe for success among "the class that mainly forms our play-going public."[70] The young and pretty Sue Beasley, a farmer's wife, agrees to hide a handsome escaped criminal from the law. When she flirts with the sheriff, her boorish husband Ira becomes insanely jealous. That night, when the sheriff stumbles out of bed to look for liquor, both Ira and the fugitive shoot and (presumably) kill him. Sue disappears into the night. Three years later, the fugitive is finally tried before Judge Lynch for murder. Ira confesses that he is the killer, but Sue returns to testify that Ira's gun had been loaded only with powder and that she has lived a chaste life since leaving him. Then, like Old Man Plunkett in *Ah Sin,* the sheriff suddenly appears to prove he is not dead after all, and the melodrama ends as Sue and Ira pledge to give their marriage another chance.[71] In the original story on which the play is based, Sue obviously has an affair with the fugitive and runs away with him after he has murdered the sheriff, although she returns to her long-suffering husband three months later. In adapting this story of sexual intrigue to the stage, Harte and Pemberton thus transformed Sue from a *femme fatale* into a plucky and much more conventional heroine.

With the actress Annie Russell in the title role, *Sue* appeared in New York and Boston throughout the fall of 1896 and in London in the spring and summer of 1898. Its reception was decidedly mixed. On the one hand, the *London Daily Telegraph* pronounced Harte "a born dramatist" (Pemberton, 273). On the other, the *New York Tribune* complained that every character in the play was "extravagant and every incident improbable," although the "numerous and propitious audience" on opening night seemed to enjoy the three hours of "chatter, melodrama, and farce."[72] On his part, Harte professed indifference to reviews: "I am quite content if the papers abuse the play so long as the audience like it, and the thing pays" (*L,* 429). He would not repeat his earlier mistake of blaming the critics for poor notices; on the contrary, he admitted they "are right in pointing out the anticlimaxes of the latter parts of the play."[73] Of course, Harte could afford to tolerate some criticism: box receipts for the play averaged more than $2,000 a week during its New York and Boston runs.[74] Frohman claimed later that "*it never paid*" (*L,* 456), that "financially it was a failure" (Booth 1944, 141) but, Harte countered, "one can hardly call a play 'a failure' which has made the amount of money that 'Sue' has."[75] The authors shared about £300 in royalties,[76] a modest first payment, Harte thought, on the income they might expect from playwriting.

He was, once again, too sanguine of success. Over the next two years, Harte and Pemberton collaborated on three more melodramas, all of them submitted to Charles Frohman, none of them produced. "I did not expect Frohman's financial experience with 'Sue' would make him look very kindly or hopefully upon any future play of ours," he conceded to Pemberton.[77] Indeed, the producer "acted very queerly" about the scripts they had written at his suggestion.[78] Personally, Harte considered *Clarence* a "better play" than *Sue,*[79] but Frohman refused to stage it in New York "because he said the war plays are overdone" and he declined to stage it in London because he had contracted to produce William Gillette's *Secret Service,* another American melodrama "on much the same lines" (*L,* 443). Their other scripts suffered similar fates. Frohman thought they contained "too many characters" to be popular "at present," and reluctantly Harte agreed. "The greatest trouble we have," he wrote Pemberton in November 1898, "is that our experience [with] 'Sue' has been so utterly confusing, conflicting and astounding that it *teaches* us nothing" and so "we have absolutely nothing to go upon by way of guide to our other ventures! We are, if we consult the notices and critiques of 'Sue,' the authors of a highly successful and much talked of play—even a distinctly 'novel' one—yet we [cannot] get an order for another from actor or manager . . . ." Harte concluded with classic understatement: "Verily a dramatist's life is not a happy one!"[80]

Ironically, Harte's own plays were never so popular or profitable as some of the pirated stagings of his stories. An adaptation of "M'liss" by Clay M. Greene starring Katy Mayhew was performed in San Francisco as early as 1877, and a musical version of the same story starring Annie Pixley opened in New York in 1880 and toured the country for several seasons until Harte took legal action to prevent it from playing in England.[81] He also vied with pirates over dramatic rights to "Tennessee's Partner" in 1895.[82] The horse opera *Salomy Jane,* based on Harte's story "Salomy Jane's Kiss" and starring Eleanor Robson, was one of the theatrical hits of 1907. No fewer than 10 silent movies were based on his works, including an adaptation of "M'liss" starring Mary Pickford (Quinn, 113; Stewart, 106, 333); and as recently as 1976 a musical version of the story was produced off Broadway. Meanwhile, most of Harte's unproduced scripts have disappeared over the years, although fragments of some drafts survive in the New York Public Library and the Beinecke Library at Yale University and a complete script of "The Luck of Roaring Camp" is owned by the U.S. Library of Congress. More than the melodramas that were produced, these lost scripts betray his shortcomings as a dramatist. "His plays were too bad for the stage, or else too good for it," as Howells remarked (*LFA,* 300). That is, Harte did not fail merely to construct coherent plots or to depict the West in convincing detail, he failed fundamentally to gauge the market for his work. In the alchemy of adaptation, he converted gold into dross, sacrificing the irony and pathos of the best of his stories to the farce he hoped would sell. However, as he at last ruefully admitted, his plays simply were "not sufficiently convincing or absorbing to an audience."[83] Like the gamblers who frequent his fiction, he had speculated in a risky business, taken the odds, overplayed his hand, and was finally "euchred."

Chapter Five
From Poker Flat to Picadilly
Literary Expatriate

Despite the "palpable loss" of his consular salary of $3,000 annually, about half of his total income (*L,* 284, 285), Harte was determined to remain abroad. "I have just begun some work which will test my ability to hold my own here," he wrote Anna in 1885. He maintained that " I can do better here than elsewhere," and he insisted "I am not staying here for pleasure." Fortunately, he added, the Van de Veldes' "kindness to me has undergone no change with my uncertain fortunes,"[1] and he became a permanent guest in their home. Fortunately, too, he had had the foresight to employ a new literary agent, A. P. Watt of Paternoster Square, in 1884: "I have a very good agent here, who looks after my interest, and to whom I pay a percentage, and who relieves me from all the horrible torments of being obliged to offer my manuscripts personally to publishers, as I used to do in America. It takes away half the pains of authorship" (*L,* 310). For better or worse, Watt had a profound influence on Harte's career by regulating the production and mass-marketing of his stories. During a period of only two months in the spring of 1885, Harte wrote about 42,000 words—"which is much for me, who am slow and not over-prolific."[2] He increased his output because, he explained, "I do not know how long my popularity will last with the public, and I must make the most of it" (*L,* 268). After leaving the Consulate in Glasgow, as he wrote Frau Schneider in January 1886, he "had more time for literary work, and I have profited by it so that I have rather *increased* then diminished my labor and my income. I make more money, but I have to work harder for it!"[3] Harte largely abandoned his "old shorter and more condensed style" (*L,* 273) and published at least one volume of new fiction every year from 1883 until 1902. Incredibly, a full two-thirds of his *oeuvre* was written during the last seventeen years of his life, after he hired Watt & Son to handle his business. By 1893 he was reportedly earning $15,000 annually, more than he made while under contract to Fields, Osgood in 1871–72; still, his monthly drafts to Anna were occasionally late because he "had not sufficient money, and had to finish some work and see my agent, before I could get it."[4] Watt touted Harte like feet in a mine sold at shares, peddling his stories by the column inch to such newspaper syndicates as Bacheller, Johnson & Bacheller, and the National Press Agency. He wrote "nothing that [was] not solicited" in advance through his agent (Haskell, 17), and he was "generally 'bespoke' for a story or two ahead" (M&M, 104).

This fiction, designed for quick sale to magazines, mostly ran along the same well-worn ruts. In "A Ship of '49" (1885), the heroine and her duplicitous lover discover a hidden treasure in the hold of a long-beached ship; she is spared the anguish of a loveless marriage when the gold coins turn out to be gilded lead disks and her suitor vamooses. Watt hawked the novella "Maruja" to both the *Illustrated London News* and *Harper's Weekly* in the summer of 1885—a twin-shilling for which Harte congratulated him: it "was managed with great tact, delicacy, and patience." He was "convinced that the commission I pay you has been fully returned by the appreciation of the market value of my work through your efforts" (*L,* 276). This story was based on a "genuine legend," or so Harte claimed,[5] about a curse placed on a plot of land expropriated from the Church. The blonde heroine Maruja Saltonstall, the child of a Hispanic woman and an "old Salem whaling captain" (I, 8), ignores the demand that she wed "one of my mother's race" (I, 15) to marry the noble Harry Guest, at once restoring the land to its historic owners, removing the curse by disproving its efficacy, and betraying Harte's persistent belief in white superiority. "Maruja" was, by critical consensus, "overdrawn and exaggerated."[6] Harte agreed it was "at best only a ghost of a ghost" of his best fiction and "may even act as a mild soporific."[7] In fact, he often bemoaned the "terrible daily grind" of literary production over the months (*L,* 354; M&M, 104; Booth 1944, 140), and he once confessed to Florence Henniker that his "writing lately has revealed to me hitherto unknown depths of weariness and stupidity."[8] Much of it, he admitted later, was "drivel" (*L,* 379). Or, as he wrote Anna, "you cannot possibly hate pen and ink as I do who live in it and by it perpetually" (*L,* 354). Still, Hay thought in mid–1886 that Harte had only begun to realize "the real maturity" of his powers (*L,* 306), and Hamlin Garland favorably reviewed *A Millionaire of Rough-and-Ready and Devil's Ford* the following year for the *Boston Transcript.*[9] In any event, in his late fiction Harte crystalized his theories of personality, race, and sexuality; recognized the racist underpinings of Manifest Destiny; and covertly alluded to some of the salient events in his private life.

Nature versus Nurture

Over the course of his career, Harte did evolve as a writer, but in a direction his early partisans would scarcely have approved. During his years abroad, as he became familiar with the ideas of Darwin and Huxley and the fiction of Zola and Hardy,[10] he fixed upon "hereditary influences" or "hereditary instinct" (XVIII, 90, 91) as the most elemental forces shaping character.

Harte's proto-naturalism is perhaps most evident in "The Ancestors of Peter Atherly" (1897), a Zolaesque (and unintentionally ludicrous) social and genealogical history of a family. The *Critic* declared in 1898 that this tale "may fitly be described as a masterpiece" and "will unquestionably rank high among [Harte's] best productions."[11] The twins Peter and Jenny Atherly are the children of an alcoholic charwoman and, ostensibly, an English aristocrat. During their overland journey to California the elder Atherlys had been "captured by Indians, who had held them captive for ten months" (XIV, 3). The twins have in fact been fathered by Silver Cloud, the chief of the tribe, although they are ignorant of their Indian ancestry. A racial atavist, Jenny betrays as a young woman the traits of an "Amazonian" savage beneath the veneer of her convent training: "She not only could dance with feverish energy all night, but next day could mount a horse—she was a fearless rider— and lead the most accomplished horsemen. She was a good shot, she walked with the untiring foot of a coyote, she threaded the woods with the instinct of a pioneer. Peter regarded her with a singular mingling of astonishment and fear. Surely she had not learned this at school!" (XIV, 18–19). During a visit to England to trace (he thinks) his family tree, Peter is similarly overcome by primitive desires: he is inexplicably tempted to "seize" the fair Lady Elfrida, a "young and innocent girl," and "bear her away—a prisoner, a hostage" on "a galloping horse in the dust of the prairie—far beyond the seas!" (XIV, 40). Obviously, in Harte's conventional view, women are more temperamental than men, less resistant to biological or hereditary impulses. Although they are twins, Jenny succumbs to the deepest longings of her nature, whereas Peter represses the aboriginal instincts welling in his breast. After his election to Congress, he learns the truth of his patrilineage from "the scornful lips" (XIV, 56) of his "real" father's friend Chief Gray Eagle during a private conversation at a state dinner. (Harte considered the idea of miscegenation so repugnant that the story opens after Silver Cloud's death. Much as Judge Driscoll is a surrogate for the dead Cecil Essex, the offending father of the usurper Tom in Twain's *Pudd'nhead*

Wilson, Gray Eagle should logically *be* the father of the Atherly twins but he appears instead merely as his "trace.") Significantly, Peter and Gray Eagle cross paths not in the West, where such a chance meeting would seem more plausible, but in a corner of the East Room of the White House, the very citadel of the Anglo (East/white) occupation force.

As a closet "half-breed," Peter Atherly becomes a champion of Indian causes. He "devoted himself and his increasing wealth" to philanthropic projects from "an infinite pity and sense of duty towards his own race" (XIV, 56). However, like Harte, who never publicly acknowledged his own Jewish ancestry, Peter resists the temptation "to openly proclaim his kinship with the despised race" (XIV, 58), a decision he justifies by a tortured rationalization: he wishes to save his sister and the blonde lawyer she has married from public derision and ostracism or worse. Ironically, however, by failing even to tell Jenny she is a mixed-blood, he unwittingly permits her to compound the problem when she becomes pregnant: "Jenny's child! Silver Cloud's grandchild! This was a complication he had not thought of. No! It was too late to tell his secret now" (XIV, 63). The issue of interracial marriage comes to a head in the final chapter of the novella, which Harte stages on a western reservation. Incredibly, Lady Elfrida (or Friddy), Peter's love interest, reappears to decry race mixing: "You wouldn't like your sister to have married an Indian, would you?" she asks. Peter insists he is free of racial bigotry: "I have even thought myself of marrying an Indian woman," he asserts (XIV, 88). He prepares a report for the government in which Harte obviously articulates his own views:

I am satisfied that much of the mischievous and extravagant prejudice against the half breed and all alliances of the white and red races springs from the ignorance of the frontiersman and his hasty generalization of facts. There is no doubt that an intermixture of blood brings out purely superficial contrasts the more strongly, and that against the civilizing habits and even costumes of the half breed, certain Indian defects appear the more strongly as in the case of the color line of the quadroon and octoroon, but it must not be forgotten that these are only the contrasts of specific improvement, and the inference that the borrowed defects of a half breed exceed the original defects of the full-blooded aborigine is utterly illogical. (XIV, 99)

Duckett concludes that "There is no doubt of [Harte's] condemnation of white men whose ignorance and prejudice produce social injustices" (Duckett 1953, 210).

However liberal his statement may have seemed in theory, Harte shrank from its implications. Peter apparently proposes marriage to Friddy and tells her his most guarded secret, but the author spares the reader the details of their delicate conversation by failing to record it. Like the mixed-bloods in "In the Carquinex Woods," moreover, the Atherly twins die in the dénouement, the only resolution the author apparently could imagine to the race problem they represent. "Consciously or unconsciously," according to Duckett, Harte "seems to support the code" or social taboo on interracial marriage (Duckett 1953, 209). Indeed, he reinforces Indian stereotypes in the manner of their deaths: Peter and Jinny are killed and scalped by savage natives, and they suffer "torture with an Indian stoicism." They are, by implication, martyrs to their race. The warriors "dipped their arrows and lances in the heroic heart's blood of their victims, and worshiped their still palpitating flesh" (XIV, 120). Their grim deaths resolve nothing but the problem of how to conclude the story.

A progressive on most social issues, Harte obviously harbored misgivings about miscegenation, which he rationalized in these late stories by reference to heredity and the hierarchy of race. His ideas were not so extreme as those of Cooper, who had warned in *The Prairie,* for example, that "half-breeds" would acquire the least desirable traits of both races. Still, Harte thought that mixed-bloods were liable to inherit the precocious sexuality of the so-called inferior races. As early as 1871, in "The Princess Bob and Her Friends," he noted that a 14-year-old Indian girl is a woman "according to the laws of her race" (XVII, 82). The hero of "At the Mission of San Carmel" (1882) declares he "preferred to have" the 15-year-old "mongrel" Juanita "for a wife than a daughter" (XVI, 308, 343). Harte also referred in "A Convert of the Mission" (1895) to "the fourteen-year-old wife" of a Mexican shopkeeper (VI, 160). Each of these tales was but a rehearsal, however, for "What Happened at the Fonda" (1899), a remarkably explicit account of sexual initiation. Its title should be read not as a declarative statement but as a question or riddle. The heroine, the fair Cota Ramierez, is the 14-year-old daughter of a "fair-skinned Spanish settler" and a Mexican woman—a "mere child," perhaps, but "those people marry at twelve," as one character insists (XI, 211, 210). Cota has only recently returned from a convent school, where she has been taught "the litany of the Virgin," to her home in the central mountains. "Grey eyed and blonde as she was in color, her racial peculiarities were distinct," Harte writes, and she rides "a mongrel mare" as "distinct and peculiar as herself" (XI, 213, 215). The analogy of calico mare and mixed-blood heroine is developed at length in this story, particularly when a young man, "a singularly good rider of untrained stock" who is "proud of his prowess" (XI, 216), mounts the horse bareback. Harte's description of the fellow astride the animal is rife with sexual double entendre; e.g., "He felt her sensitive spine arch like a cat's beneath him" and he "allowed his body to rise with her spring" (XI, 217). As Jeffrey F. Thomas notes, the mare, "Little-used to being ridden and dangerous to men, somehow embodies the ripening sexual power" of the lovely Cota, who is vicariously initiated. "Only such an interpretation can explain Harte's insistence on so many details" of "the bizarre affinity" between girl and horse (Thomas, 106).

As this story may suggest, Harte excelled at the portrayal of child characters. Indeed, he was acclaimed by many of his contemporaries as second only to Dickens among writers of fiction about children. In "The Luck of Roaring Camp," according to one reviewer, Harte had studied childhood "with a closeness, and delineated [it] with a force and beauty" unique to the age. "The picture of that little child, left motherless amongst a set of rough, wild Western miners, who became gradually civilized and softened by the influence of the tender, innocent little presence amongst them, was drawn with a power and pathos which at once established" Harte's fame.[12] Similarly, the *Overland Monthly* for January 1887 praised his "almost feminine knowledge and appreciation of children";[13] and the *New York Times,* in its notice of his last collection of stories in 1902, opined that Harte's child characters "are a perennial delight. They are unhampered by tradition and timidity. . . . They have experiences and revelations quite their own."[14] Almost all modern critics of Harte's works share similar views on at least this one point: Joseph Harrison opined that he "frequently wrote well when he was dealing with children" (Harrison, 409); Arthur Hobson Quinn and George Stewart commended him for his "love of children" (Quinn, 234; Stewart, 45, 316); and Margaret Duckett noted his "intuitive" sympathy for children (Duckett 1964, 328). However, such comments as these overlook the reason child types recur throughout Harte's fiction: often such stories are case studies in the "nature versus nurture" debate.

In his early work, Harte entered this debate on the side of the environmentalists. "I often fancied I detected" among children born and raised in California, he remarks in 1866, "a coarseness of fiber and precocity of growth which belonged to a country of mammoth strawberries, and fruit-bearing trees only a foot high. Talking with them, you will find a readiness of expression and quick self-assertion which seems to be appropriate to a country where spring is born full grown, like Minerva." Harte had the impression that, were he to give one of these children a half-dollar, it would not be spent on sweets but "laid away for a future investment" (*BHC*, 93). As if to underscore the analogy between children and vegetables, Harte published a sketch in 1862 about a young San Francisco street Arab named Melons and his young crony Carrots (XVII, 199–209).

These remarks may serve to gloss several characters in his early tales. In "The Luck of Roaring Camp" (1868), for example, little Tommy Luck thrives during the first months of his brief life in the "invigorating climate" of the California gold fields: "Nature took the foundling to her broader breast. In that rare atmosphere of the Sierra foothills—that air pungent with balsamic odor, that ethereal cordial at once bracing and exhilarating—he may have found food and nourishment, or a subtle chemistry that transmuted ass's milk to lime and phosphorus." As in the case of Hawthorne's Pearl, "Nature was his nurse and playfellow" (VII, 9, 15). The young pupils of the schoolmarm in "The Idyl of Red Gulch" romp in the woods "because they had not yet grown quite away from the breast of the bounteous Mother" (VII, 80). If Harte's boys are budding stockbrokers or bank tellers in training, his California girls are plump and voluptuous, vegetables ripe for the picking. In "The Outcasts of Poker Flat" (1869), Piney Woods, "a stout, comely damsel of fifteen," has finally eloped with her lover Tom Simson after a long engagement (VII, 25); the young heroine of "The Rose of Tuolumne" (1874) exhibits certain "wild habits" that survive "transplanting and cultivation" (XVI, 2); and the young hero of *Gabriel Conroy* (1876) marries a woman after a "very brief courtship," which excited no surprise "in a climate where the harvest so promptly followed the sowing" (*GC* I, 186). As late as 1878, Harte commented on "the extreme self-assertion and early maturity of American children" (XXIV, 517).

His story "M'liss," first published in 1860 and revised in 1863, betrays the more sinister implications of this idea that California children, especially girls, are naturally precocious. With "her plump white arm," "round curves," and "plump white shoulders," 15-year-old Clytemnestra Morpher is an "early bloomer," a trait Harte attributes in no small part to "the climatic laws of the Red Mountain region" of the Sierra Nevada (*Outcasts*, 41, 47, 70). Melissa Smith, the prepubescent heroine, is at the tender age of 10 no less sexually advanced than Clytie, especially in the original version of the story. Indeed, the original "M'liss" seems, at least in this context, nothing less than a study in pedophilia. Harte repeatedly hints of the heroine's devotion to her young schoolmaster, and of his affection for her—they walk hand in hand through the forest, and at one point she gives him "a fierce little kiss" (VII, 162, 167). The story ends as the master in effect proposes to his "passionate little" pupil:

Seizing her hands in his and looking full into her truthful eyes, he said,—
    "Lissy, will you go with *me?*"
The child put her arms around his neck, and said joyfully, "Yes."
    "But now—to-night?"
    "To-night."
And, hand in hand, they passed into the road,—the narrow road that had once brought her weary feet to the master's door, and which it seemed she should not tread again alone. (VII, 183)

In his 1863 revision of the story, Harte would delete the most salacious of these passages; and he would even disinter the orphan Melissa's long-lost mother, a beautiful 30-year-old woman who becomes the master's new potential love interest. In other words, Harte would radically revise the story to obscure the earlier suggestions of sexual impropriety. Over the course of the next 40 years, Harte would repeatedly rewrite the basic plot of "M'liss"—a sexual fantasy involving an older teacher and a female student, a male authority figure and an adolescent girl.

In his later stories, Harte rarely attempted to attribute the precocious sexuality of children to the influence of climate and soil. Instead, he qualified his earlier environmentalism by emphasizing the instinctive or inherited sex traits of his young characters. His descriptions of natural landscape were never again so vivid and detailed as they had been in his most popular and memorable stories. More than a few reviewers complained of the "vagueness" of his scenery.[15] This shift in his perspective may begin to explain the difference most readers sense between those tales written while he was living in California, and his later fiction, especially after he sailed for Europe and permanent exile. That is, Harte was increasingly alienated from his subject. Much as he invented an ever-more-mythological California as a setting for his stories after he left the state, he filled his increasingly contrived plots with mere caricatures of miners, gamblers, and children. In these late stories, moreover, blood will tell, usually in bestial metaphor and often in prurient detail.

Harte gave a new twist to his increasingly formulaic treatment of adolescent girls in "Cressy" (1888), another story about a child sed- uctress à la Flip Fairley who is courted by her schoolmaster, the basic premise of the original "M'liss." In her facial features Cressy McKinstry "appeared [to be] a girl of fifteen," Harte writes, although "in her developed figure and the maturer drapery of her full skirts she seemed a woman" (XXIV, 26–27). She wears "a long, clinging coarse blue gown, that accented the graceful curves of her slight, petticoat-less figure" (XXIV, 47). Her "rounded arms, "pretty shoulders," "length of limb and the long curves of her neck and back" are the result of "thorough breeding" (XXIV, 103, 116). As her father explains to her Yankee teacher, her sexual appetite was whetted at an early age: "She was a grownd girl fit to marry afore she was a child. She had young fellers a-sparkin' her afore she ever played with 'em ez boy and girl" (XXIV, 63). Oscar Wilde, no less, would describe Cressy as "the most tantalising of heroines," "a wonderful nymph" who "has in her some- thing of Artemis, and not a little of Aphrodite." Her teacher is no pedophile, Harte is quick to note: at age 20, he is "scarcely her senior" (XXIV, 72). Lest he be accused of promoting immorality between "master and pupil," moreover, Harte interrupts the story to decry their "foolish dream" of romance (XXIV, 121). Still, master and pupil share a "mutual passion" (XXIV, 122, 203), or so it seems. They hug-dance together "in such perfect rhythm and unison" they are "scarcely con- scious of motion," and they literally roll in the hay in the McKinstry barn (XXIV, 120, 186). Cressy professes love for the master at first sight: "We love each other, we belong to each other," she whispers in his ear (XXIV, 219). But, like Harte's "heathen Chinee," she has "ways that are dark" and "tricks that are vain." She may be merely a flirt and a tease after all. "It is difficult to say whether she sacrifices herself on the altar of romance," Wilde suggests, "or is merely a girl with an extraordinary sense of humour."[16] In the end, she jilts the teacher with whom she has trifled and marries a neighbor boy more nearly her own age. "Cressy, much as I loved her," Harte admitted, "turned her back upon me at the last moment, and skipped out of my pages with a man I had only just introduced to her!" (L, 347).

One of Harte's last stories, "The Pupil of Chestnut Ridge" (1902), epitomizes his tendency, more pronounced over time, to link race or ethnicity to sexual maturity. This tale is yet another variation on

"M'liss": a male teacher is again attracted to a young female student, in this case an orphan aptly named Concepcion or "Concha" for short. (The Spanish nickname suggests the vaginally-symbolic conch shell.) "She's—she's a trifle dark complected," her adoptive mother tells the schoolmaster.

> "She is n't a nigger nor an Injin, ye know, but she's kinder a half-Spanish, half-Mexican Injin, what they call 'mes——mes——' "
> "Mestiza," suggested Mr. Brooks; "a half-breed or mongrel." (IV, 215)

Concha is "goin' on twelve," but the report of her age only serves to unnerve the teacher. He broods upon "the precocious maturity of the mixed races" and even recalls having seen "brides of twelve and mothers of fourteen among the native villagers" to the south (IV, 218). Predictably, on Concha's first day in school, he is "struck" by her "already womanly" figure (IV, 220). Like the adolescent heroines of Harte's other late stories, she is "a singular combination of the spoiled child and the coquettish señorita" (IV, 222). Although in this tale Harte ostensibly satirizes the "foolish" race prejudices of the Southwestern emigrants (IV, 216, 224), he repeatedly compromises the satire, even referring twice to Concha's "languid indifference" to study which, according to the author, is a trait specific "to her race" (IV, 226, 227). The teacher's worst fears (or fondest hopes?) are realized one day at recess when he spies Concha in the woods beyond the schoolyard at the center of a circle of children as she dances "that most extravagant feat of the fandango—the audacious sembicuaca" with its seductive moves and poses (IV, 229). The story ends abruptly on the next page when Concha elopes with a Spanish vaquero. "We were deceived," her mother tells the teacher. "She was a grown woman—accordin' to these folks' ways and ages" (IV, 229–30). Rather than propose a solution to the problem of prejudice against mixed-bloods, according to Duckett, Harte here throws up his hands in despair (Duckett 1953, 211). Such a conclusion was the dark flower of his belief that biology is destiny. If the children in Harte's early works seem soft and impressionable to the imprint of nature, the girls in his late fiction seem little more than adolescent types of such "fallen women" as Nana Coupeau, Maggie Johnson, and Carrie Meeber. If he wrote his early tales in the so-called Dickensian mode, his later works betray the influence of Zola and Hardy and presage the naturalism of Crane and Dreiser.

Anti-Imperialism

Politically, Harte was a mugwump, a liberal Republican, although by his own admission he became "more radical" rather than "conservative with years" (L, 231). He sympathized with the "poor starving devils of unemployed labourers" who rioted in the streets of London during the winter of 1885–86: "I have seen [the English upper classes] brought face to face . . . with the howling, starving mob they and their fathers have trodden upon and despised for all these years, and they have grown pale" (L, 302). He again denounced the "one-idead stupidity of the governing classes" and cheered the "feeble revolutions of Trafalgar Square" in a letter to Hay the following winter (M&M, 105). Whereas in such early tales as "The Legend of Monte del Diablo" and "The Right Eye of the Commander" he had betrayed a rather benign view of American and Spanish colonialism, in several late stories he decried the notion of manifest destiny. "I am an earnest Republican—and I think a *just* one," he reminded Anna in September 1887, "but I can understand how a man feels when he is a Communist and a Socialist—and what makes him one!" (L, 321). Harte was, at the time, writing "The Crusade of the Excelsior" for the *Illustrated London News.* The story "is on new ground and has an original idea as its foundation," he claimed (L, 314). A dystopian fantasy, it belies Stanley T. Williams's assertion that Harte never commented "on American imperialism, or on agricultural and industrial dynamics in relation to the archaic system of the [Spanish] missions" (Williams, 233). In this story, which is broadly modeled on the career of the American filibusterer William Walker, Harte repeatedly condemns racial and class injustices and endorses the right to self-determination of oppressed and colonized nations.

En route to California in 1854 with a congress of characters abroad, the barque *Excelsior*—Harte borrows the name from Longfellow's poem about a youth who perishes in an avalanche while on a mysterious quest—is caught in a fog and carried by the wind and current into the Mexican port of Todos Santos (All Saints), "a sort of Sleepy Hollow" (IV, 161) or Latin American Shangri-La entirely isolated from the rest of the world. "For fifty years the Presidio and the Mission of Todos Santos . . . have [been hidden] by impenetrable fogs from the ocean pathway at their door, cut off by burning and sterile deserts from the surrounding country. . . . [The citizens] have preserved a trust and propagated a faith in enforced but not unhappy seclusion. The wars that have shaken mankind, the dissensions that have even disturbed the serenity of their own nation on the mainland, have never reached them here. Left to themselves, they have created a blameless Arcadia and an ideal community within an extent of twenty square leagues" (IV, 52). The passengers are abandoned on shore when the suave revolutionary Leonidas Bolivar Perkins (read, Walker) incites the crew to mutiny and they sail away to aid an insurgency in a neighboring province. The company of castaway Americans quickly divides into rival cliques. The businessmen Crosby, Banks, Winslow, and Brace, entrepreneurs eager to exploit the natural and human resources of Todos Santos for profit, are recognized as "Legitimists," heirs to the Anglo "brigands" who "invaded California" (IV, 104). The liberal opposition, including the Boston suffragist and intellectual Susan Markham, is led by "the goddess-like and beautiful" Eleanor Keene, whom the natives regard as a "young agitator of revolutions" (IV, 79, 115); and the melancholy gadfly James Hurlstone, whose iconoclastic surname suggests his role in the resistance to both the radical leftist Perkins and the capitalists arrayed on the right. The same dialectic marks local politics in Todos Santos, with such rebels as Martinez and Ruiz, under the influence of Thomas Paine, fulminating against the power of established authority, particularly the Catholic Church, to subvert the popular will: the Franciscan priests "will not accept, they will not proclaim the Republic to the people" (IV, 161). These "one-idead" men—the phrase is the same one Harte used in his letter to Hay to describe the English governing classes—are "devoted to the conversion of the heathen" rather than to improving the peasants' lot (IV, 102).

Keene and Hurlstone are, it seems, the only meliorists in the novella. During their months of forced exile in Todos Santos, she teaches English "to the Comandante's flock" of youngsters at the Presidio while he designs and builds an Indian school. He even proposes to integrate the Mission school, to allow "his flock" of "half-breed" children to "mingle with the pure-blooded races on an equality," a heretical notion the priest Padre Esteban judges "the revolutionary idea of this *sans culotte* reformer" (IV, 182). This episode, according to Duckett, underscores "Harte's opposition to the practice of keeping people in ignorance and curtailing human rights in order to maintain orthodoxy."[17] Hurlstone's "quiet, unselfish work" among the "heathen" also endears him to Eleanor Keene, who contrasts it with the "lower aims and listless pleasures" of the other stranded passengers of the *Excelsior* (IV, 182–83). Predictably, of course, they fall in love despite a forbidding complication: like Harte, Hurlstone is a fugitive from an unhappy marriage. "I knew that the shackles I had deliberately forged could not be loosened except by death" (IV, 96), he once declares. The character of Hurlstone's wife is based not on Anna Harte, however, but on Adah Isaacs Menken, the poet and popular stage actress best known for her leading role in "Mazeppa," whom the author remembered from "the old California days" (L, 321). After this "star of nudity" (IV, 97) is reported to have died of exhaustion, drugs, and Panama fever in the penultimate chapter, however, Hurlstone is free to marry Keene after all. This ludicrous subplot is, in all, the least satisfactory feature of the tale. "There is no necessity for such a writer as Bret Harte to stoop to such cheap devices, tricks smelling strongly of the amateur domestic drama," the *Boston Transcript* sniffed.[18]

After simmering for some 200 pages, the story finally comes to a boil with the reappearance in Todos Santos of Senor Perkins, the peripatetic adventurer and so-called Liberator of Quinquinambo. Like a catalyst in a chemical reaction, Perkins returns at "the invitation of certain distressed patriots" to "assist them in the deliverance from the effete tyranny of the Church and its Government" (IV, 218). Although sympathetic (like Harte) to the cause of reform, Hurlstone respects the clerical government of Todos Santos as the duly constituted authority and scorns the rebels as "malcontents" and their "unholy crusade" as a "pot-house rebellion" (IV, 231, 221). The bloodless revolution occurs on schedule the next day, its success seemingly guaranteed by a feckless and "fickle garrison" of soldiers who immediately reappoint their former commander to the office of "Generalissimo under the new régime." The people of Todos Santos, a "harmless race" of virtual "children" (IV, 186), respond to their liberation with a bestial display: "A surging mob of vacant and wondering peons, bearing a singular resemblance to the wild cattle and horses which intermingled with them in blind and unceasing movement across the Plaza and up the hilly street, and seemingly as incapable of self-government, were alternately dispersed and stampeded or allowed to gather again as occasion required. Some of these heterogeneous bands were afterwards found—the revolution accomplished—gazing stupidly on the sea, or ruminating in bovine wantonness on the glacis before the Presidio" (IV, 230). Despite his best-laid plans for a *coup d'état* and a Central American confederacy, Perkins fails to anticipate a back-room alliance of local radicals with American businessmen, and in consequence he is forced to abandon his military strategy. As Mrs. Markham had earlier observed, "From first to last we've underrated [the people of Todos Santos], forgetting they are in the majority" (IV, 122). Like William Walker in Honduras (and Harte's Peter Schroeder in Ometeppe), Perkins is arrested and executed by firing squad. While the nation is saved from Perkins's brand of iron-fisted tyranny, it does not simply revert to its isolationism and complacency. "Under the truly catholic shelter of its veranda Padre Esteban and the heretic stranger mingled harmoniously, and the dissensions of local and central Government were forgotten," Harte announces in the end. The insidious American capitalists are banished, to be sure, but Hurlstone and Keene are invited to remain and manage the ranches and mines they purchase "from their proscribed countrymen" (IV, 249). As a result of their progressive business practices, Todos Santos enlists in the community of nations: its port "was henceforth open to all commerce, the firm of Hurlstone & Keene long retained the monopoly of trade, and was a recognized power of intelligent civilization and honest progress on the Pacific coast" (IV, 250). The solution Harte envisions to the related problems of economic exploitation and social unrest is typically timid—benign modernization through commercial trade, a kind of Better Business code—although the story as a whole betrays remarkable insight into the plight of developing countries with traditional cultures threatened by the expansionist designs of American industry. As might be expected, "The Crusade of the Excelsior" sailed into a critical squall: the *Times* of London thought it "unsatisfactory" and "perplexing,"[19] for example. The *Independent* complained that, while it was "readable," the plot was "confused,"[20] and the *New York Tribune* derided its "absence of *vraisemblance.*"[21]

Little more than a decade later, during the Spanish–American War, Harte would again assail the notion of manifest destiny and, indirectly, the wars of conquest it sanctioned. He would ridicule jingoism in the grimly humorous "Uncle Juba," the ballad of an aging Southern black man sent "to Cuba wid de odder boys in blue" not because he is a fit combatant but merely because he is immune to "all fevers dat dey knew."

> I can tackle yaller fever all de day,
> I'm de only man for Cuba what can stay,
> For agin de bery worst kind of malaria
> Dat dey knew—dey knew,
> I'm an iron-plated, sheathed and belted area
>   Froo and froo—all froo.

While other soldiers in Cuba "died like flies" from so-called embalmed beef, Uncle Ju "took his rations straight." Yet he dies anyway when, in the final stanza, he is shot by "a Spanish gunner" (Kozlay, 422–24). Similarly, "Three Vagabonds of Trinadad" (1900) is set in a fictional frontier settlement whose name Harte apparently selected for its Caribbean associations. Its citizens, unlike many of Harte's contemporaries, do not "dream of Expansion and Empire," although the xenophobic town father Parkin Skinner preaches the same doctrine of Anglo-Saxon superiority as the yellow press and other warmongers of the 1890s: "this is a white man's country," he declares, and the "nigger of every description . . . hez to clar off of God's footstool when the Anglo-Saxon get started! . . . It's our manifest destiny to clar them out— that's what we was put here for—and it's just the work we've got to do!" (X, 220–21). Infected with this virulent strain of racism, his adolescent son Bob becomes a "little white tyrant" who is "selfish" and "brutal" to his Chinese and Indian playmates Li Tee and Jim (X, 226). Because Bob wastes food, Li Tee dies of starvation. Because Bob lies to his father that the Indian "stoled his gun," Jim is shot and killed as a renegade. Each of them is a victim of the hatred spread by the white supremacist Skinner, whose surname summarizes his entire ideology. The same presumption of racial superiority, Harte implies, abetted American imperialism at the end of the century.

Trilogy

Harte was, quite literally, writing himself to death by the early 1890s. He had approached John Hay after Benjamin Harrison's election as president in 1888 about "getting a [consular] post again over here" in anticipation of "the coming time when this pen will be supplanted by younger and better ones" (M&M, 107), but his prospects were apparently so dismal he soon dropped the subject. "I have nothing but this wretched hand of mine—already growing weaker by age—to support us year by year," he complained to Anna in mid–1892. Still, he discouraged her from moving to England: "we should certainly run in debt" as a result of the additional expense. "Poverty is dreadful anywhere," he warned her. "Here, among strangers, it is terrible."[22] Of course, he was far from poverty-stricken. His slavishness to fashion was, in fact, legendary in London social circles. Gertrude Atherton saw him about this time at the American Embassy in London and described him later as a "dapper dandified little man, who walked with short mincing steps, as if his patent leather shoes were too small for him."[23] Henry Dam remarked in 1894 that "his attire exhibits a nicety of detail which, in a man whose dignity and sincerity were less impressive, would seem foppish" (Dam, 39). Harte was "a charming man to meet," according to George Newell Lovejoy in 1895, though he was "somewhat given to fads" such as matching his socks and cravat.[24] From all indications, he lived within his income, but barely.

To tap the lucrative serial market—and incidentally to prove his ability to "write a story beyond a certain length" (M&M, 104)—Harte wrote a trilogy of short novels: "A Waif of the Plains" (1889), "Susy" (1893), and "Clarence" (1894). First published serially under the auspices of the S. S. McClure syndicate in the Sunday editions of papers such as the *New York Sun, Philadelphia Inquirer, Chicago Inter–Ocean,* and *New Orleans Times–Democrat,* this trilogy "marks the high point of his later career," according to Donald E. Glover.[25] In "Waif," young Clarence Brant is a type of American Adam, an innocent outcast like Robin in Hawthorne's "My Kinsman, Major Molineux" who is repeatedly abandoned to his fate by parental figures and other adults. An "orphan put on the [wagon] train at 'St. Jo' by some relative of his stepmother, to be delivered to another relative at Sacramento" in 1852 (II, 160), Clarence and his young friend Susy, a "small Eve" (II, 199), escape an Indian massacre when they are accidentally separated from the wagons in the middle of the prairie. After they are rescued by another band of emigrants, Susy is adopted by the wealthy Judge Peyton and his wife, while Clarence is consigned to the streets, left alone to search for his cousin. Only one person—a mysterious miner named Flynn, apparently on the lam from the law—helps him locate the "oldish, half-foreign-looking man" who purports to be his relation (II, 240). Their alleged "tie of kinship" is "tacitly ignored by both" of them (II, 243), and after three years Clarence enrolls in the Jesuit college in San Jose. Only on the last page does he learn the truth about his past from Father Sobriente, the school principal: his father, Colonel Hamilton Brant of Louisville, abandoned his family, moved west, turned to crime, and changed his name. "This man Flynn," the priest intones, "*was your father!*" (II, 260). Although he has finally been killed in Mexico "as an insurgent" (II, 259), presumably a mercenary, "Flynn" has bequeathed a fortune to the son he had dared not own in life. In dying, he has both orphaned and acknowledged Clarence, who decrees he will "keep my father's name" (II, 261). The moment marks his assumption of manhood and ends the first third of the trilogy.

Harte traced Clarence's romantic misadventures in "Susy," the next story in the series. (He obviously lost interest in the title character, a spoiled and petulant brat who plays only a minor role.) Although he is the son of an assassin and pirate, Clarence is not a criminal by birth. Though he is aggressive and independent like his father, he has inherited the moral nature of his sainted mother. After the Judge's murder, he spends his entire inheritance to forestall Mrs. Peyton's eviction from her ranch on the basis of a forged Spanish land grant. Indeed, Clarence gradually wins the widow's trust and love: this is the plot in a nutshell. In chapter 1, Mrs. Peyton regards him as a "common creature" with "wretched" friends (VII, 10). When she disparages Hispanics as a "lazy race of mongrels," he reproves her and earns her respect. He "quickly and earnestly" explained how "it was impossible" for her in her "present relations to the natives to judge them, or to be judged by them fairly" (VII, 116, 117). Susy, the putative heroine, virtually disappears from the story after chapter 5. Clarence has fallen deeply in love with her adoptive mother by chapter 9, and he confesses his love to her in the twelfth and last chapter: "I have thought of, dreamed of, worshiped, and lived for no other woman. Even when I found Susy again, grown up here at your side; even when I thought that I might, with your consent, marry her, it was that I might be with *you* always; that I might be a part of *your* home, your family, and have a place with her in *your* heart; for it was you I loved, and *you* only" (VII, 255–56). Given the 15-year difference in their ages, Mrs. Peyton protests that any union between them would be "so wild,—so mad! so—so—utterly ridiculous!" (VII, 259). Of course, she overcomes her scruples on the final page and invites him to remain with her: "you never could leave me here alone and defenseless" (VII, 264). The *San Francisco Chronicle* commended Harte for his "delicate" portrayal of the "wooing of Peyton's widow by young Brant" given the "dangerous incongruities" of the situation.[26]

Although Susy gives her name to the story, she is displaced by Mrs. Peyton from its center. The reason? Harte inscribed in the text some of the complications in his own life in 1892–93. That is, the story reflects the author's conflicted relations at the time with Anna Harte and Mme. Van de Velde. This explanation is admittedly speculative, but wholly consistent with the available evidence. Harte did not plot his late stories in advance; on the contrary, he began with "a few characters and a situation in my mind. I let *them* work out the plot in *their* own lines and generally find they do it better than I can!"[27] Clarence is clearly a version of the author, even down to his "curling" mustache (VII, 120; Dam, 39). Much as Clarence tells the impetuous Susy she has changed "more than in looks" before he "loosed the bonds of his old companionship" with her (VII, 76, 200), Harte had ended his failed marriage to Anna in all but the legal sense. More to the point, much as Clarence is drawn to the refined Mrs. Peyton, Harte was attracted to the sophisticated Mme. Van de Velde. (The details of their relations are, for better or worse, lost in a biographical blindspot. While they corresponded as early as 1880, their letters simply have not survived, with two exceptions.) Much as Judge Peyton dies in "Susy," Count Van de Velde succumbed to influenza on 7 February 1892, shortly before Harte began to write the story. Just as Mrs. Peyton found the Judge's "affairs . . . to be greatly in disorder" after his death, Mme. Van de Velde had to untangle "the Count's affairs" (*L,* 364).

As long as Van de Velde was alive, Harte might pass as a guest in the home. With his death, Harte's status changed overnight. The widow, his amaneunsis and collaborator, was a respectable woman and the mother of nine, and Harte initially planned to find other accommodations when she "move[d] to a new house" (*L,* 367–68). However, he moved *with* her to Lancaster Gate in mid–1893, and he would reside in her home more or less to the end of his life. Their irregular relationship apparently occasioned "a more definite break with his wife," as Stewart tactfully allows. Harte continued to send her the monthly draft, but his notes were more perfunctory. If "the old arrangement seemed strange, perhaps equivocal, the new one must have seemed to the man of the world—unequivocal. Mrs. Harte could probably have gained a decree in any divorce court" (Stewart, 306). To be sure, there is no firm evidence extant that Harte and Mme. Van de Velde were lovers, although Hamlin Garland heard gossip to this effect during a visit to London (Barnett, 349), and Mark Twain bluntly claimed Harte was "kept" by the widow (*MTE,* 282). Read in this context, many passages in "Susy" seem transparently autobiographical, as if Harte were trying to rationalize the appearance of impropriety. As Clarence prepares to depart the Peyton ranch after the Judge's death, for example, he declares to the "mistress of these lands where I am only steward": "I loved you when I came here,—even when your husband was alive. Don't be angry, Mrs. Peyton; *he* would not, and need not, have been angry" (VII, 256, 257). Like Clarence, Harte would be invited to remain in the home of the widow rather than "enter the world again and seek his fortune elsewhere" (VII, 260).

The happy ending to "Susy" would unravel in the opening pages of "Clarence," the final novella in the trilogy. The hero and the former Mrs. Peyton are married scarcely a year before the widow becomes a scold and shrew. Alice—Harte finally gives her a first name—is, regretably, "a Southerner, a born slaveholder, and a secessionist" (XVIII, 4), a traitor who secedes from their union like a Confederate state the day the Civil War erupts. Clarence sides with the North, Alice with the Rebellion. Susy, who resurfaces in this story as Clarence's confidant, assures him "you never really liked her" after all (XVIII, 82). In the second part of the story, some four years later, Brant (rhymes with Grant) is the youngest brigadier-general in the army, a rank he has attained largely as the result of "hereditary influences," specifically the "cold blood of his father" coursing through his veins (VIII, 90, 91). Alice, on the other hand, is a mendacious Southern spy. When, in one of a series of wildly improbable scenes, she is captured by Clarence's regiment and they face off in the guardhouse, she "seemed to him no longer the Diana of his youthful fancy, but some Pallas Athene" (XVIII, 187). Fortunately, she had "borne him no child" to whom his "dreadful heritage could be again transmitted" (XVIII, 214). Ironically, she is killed by rebel soldiers while trying to escape across the lines disguised as a black woman. "Perhaps it was part of the inconsistency of her sex," Harte adds, "that she was pierced with the bullets of those she had loved, and was wearing the garments of the race she had wronged" (XVIII, 218). Although he had planned for years to depict the Rebellion in a "work of serious import" (Dam, 50), this section of the novella, as the *New York Times* concluded, is "assuredly not in Harte's best vein."[28] Indeed, it illustrates perfectly Daniel Aaron's observation that the Civil War "was not so much unfelt as unfaced" by American writers.[29] In the sensational conclusion to the story, Clarence crosses paths with Miss Faulkner, a Southern belle "greatly petted in governmental circles" around Washington for "sacrificing fidelity to flag" (XVIII, 248). By her testimony, he is exonerated of a charge of fraternizing with the enemy—that is, with his wife—during a private audience with Abraham Lincoln in the White House. Whereas in the first chapter of "Clarence" the firing on Fort Sumter dissolves both the Union and the hero's marriage to the rebel sympathizer Alice, in the last chapter the armistice both heals the nation and permits his union with the Southern loyalist Miss Faulkner, the third heroine in as many stories. "I am *so* glad it[']s done!" Harte wrote Mary Boyd the day he finished the manuscript. "It[']s five or six thousand words longer than I contemplated. And yet it ends as abruptly [as a] sneeze."[30] Despite its patriotic theme, the story was received less favorably in America than in England, where reviewers praised it as "superbly told" and "as fine a bit of work as Bret Harte has ever done."[31]

Yuba Bill and Jack Hamlin *Redivivus*

Harte returned to his earlier, more abridged and understated style in two 1893 tales that feature his old *Overland Monthly* characters and that are still occasionally anthologized: "An Ingénue of the Sierras" and "A Protégée of Jack Hamlin's." George Stewart thought they were Harte's "best stories [in] nearly twenty years" (Stewart, 305), and Joseph B. Harrison was "amazed" to discover "that Harte could have written such a pair of stories as late as 1893 and have written them so well" (Harrison, xxxi). In the first, Yuba Bill becomes the unwitting butt of an elaborate scheme by the mysterious Ingénue, the moll of the highwayman Ramon Martinez. A passenger abroad Bill's stagecoach, she appears to be a "simple and guileless" country girl who has run away from home to marry her beau. Bill resolves to help her elope, despite her fiance's rumored affiliations with the Martinez gang, because her "girlish curiosity was quite touching, and her innocence irresistible" (XX, 67). He even insists that the express company ship her trunks through to Sacramento, where the Ingénue and her husband are headed. When he "waltzes in to pervide for a young couple jest startin' in life," Bill brags, "thar's nothin' mean about [my] style, you bet" (XX, 81). Though her lover Charley Byng betrays "a certain half-shamed, half-defiant suggestion in his expression," the Ingénue's "frank, joyous, innocent face" reconciled the other passengers to "the fellow's shortcomings" (XX, 83). One of them, a judge, officiates at their wedding at a way station. Harte then transforms this deceptively innocuous romance into a *tour de force* of mistaken appearances by giving it the surprise ending of an O. Henry story. Nothing about the couple is as it seems. Beneath the frilly lace in her luggage, the Ingénue is smuggling the Martinez gang's booty in flake gold to a city assay office. Not only has she enlisted Bill's unknowing complicity in her plot, she has coerced "Byng" (read, Martinez)[32] into marrying her. As D. M. McKeithan explains, she "had him over the barrel and was offering him the choice of marrying her quietly or losing the gold and possibly going to jail."[33] Martinez has been deceived no less than he, as Bill realizes: "He's tied up to that lying little she-devil, hard and fast!" (XX, 92). At least one contemporary reviewer agreed the piece "gleams here and there with [Harte's] old-time brilliancy."[34]

The same tribute might be paid to "Protégée," another story of courtship, albeit a more self-reflexive one from which the humor has been distilled. Here a young woman has been deserted by her faithless lover, a "brother gambler" to the laconic Hamlin. "With the abstract morality of this situation Jack was not in the least concerned" until he realizes the woman is about to leap from the saloon deck of a steamer into the paddlewheel (XX, 2). After he saves her life—merely by initiating a conversation with her—he takes her under his wing, introducing her as his niece. They are, of course, birds of a feather: he is, as a gambler, as disreputable as Sophy is disgraced. His "infelix reputation"—Harte had used this same phrase to describe Hamlin in "Brown of Calaveras" a generation earlier—"made it impossible for him to assist her" except by stealth. "He who had for years faced the sneers and half-frightened opposition of the world dared not tell the truth to this girl" (XX, 28). Because she had been seduced by Ned Stratton, Sophy must impersonate a genteel young lady in order to be considered one, and Hamlin must lie in order to help her. Whereas "Ingénue" is awash in ambiguity and false appearances, the reader of "Protégée" is privy to the myriad deceptions from the beginning. Harte rails against sexual mores that stigmatize women as "loose" when, in fact, they are exploited; and he suggests Sophy's and Jack's impostures are but a form of discretion after all. The plot formula about the "fallen woman" is common enough, even as Hamlin realizes, "in cheap novelettes, in the police reports, in the Sunday papers" (XX, 10); but in this instance it achieves a certain poignancy.

Hamlin is, as usual, an ambiguous and unconventional hero. However crude his "ideas of morality" may be, his "convictions on points of honor were singularly direct and positive" (XX, 33). He simply refuses to play the part of gallant hero in this "idiotic situation" (XX, 11). To be sure, he places Sophy in a respectable boarding school "surrounded by a high white picket fence" in "the best quarter of Sacramento" (XX, 17–18), and later he sets her up in an art studio. But he is unable to tell her "frankly who he was and what was his reputation." He is gradually convinced, however, "that in his present attitude towards her he was not unlike that hound Stratton, and that, however innocent his own intent, there was a sickening resemblance to the situation on the boat in the base advantage he had taken of her friendlessness" (XX, 27–28). Meanwhile, he enters into a low intrigue with "what appeared to be a respectable, matter-of-fact woman" who dragged her "clean skirts and rustic purity after [his] heels into various places and various situations not so clean, rural, or innocent" (XX, 45, 46–47). This woman turns out to be Sophy's sister Marianne, the very person in all the world Sophy believes she has disgraced by eloping with Stratton. In the end, all the deceptions cancel out: Stratton is killed, presumably by an outraged husband; Sophy learns Hamlin is something less than a saint; Marianne learns he is something more than a *roué* and a gambler; the sisters are reconciled; and Hamlin flees both of them on the down boat.

He reappears in "Mr. Jack Hamlin's Mediation" (1899) to save the marriage of a devout rancher and his wife, a former casino dancer in San Francisco. As in the best of the stories in which he figures, Hamlin mediates between the forces of bucolic nature and corrupt civilization, typified here by Josh Rylands and the former Nell Montgomery. Initially, they seem utterly incompatible. But Nell has renounced her past ways, much as Josh has "found grace," and she is more devoted to her husband than he is to the Lord. "You've got a wife a d——d sight truer to you for what you call her 'sin,'" Hamlin tells him, "than you've ever been to her, with all your d——d salvation" (XII, 56). By the end of the tale, they have reconciled and had a baby, figuratively the child of Hamlin's mediation.

Had Harte but passed all his late tales through the same sluice as these three. Most consist instead of slag with only an occasional flake of color. "A Maecenas of the Pacific Slope" (1890), for example, celebrates the exploits of a mysterious millionaire financier, a proto-Gatsby in boots and spurs, who saves his fortune in mining stocks through a timely merger with the heroine. In "The Reformation of James Reddy" (1893), the hero is rescued from poverty and dissipation by hard work and the love of a good woman, though Harte takes a page from Frank Stockton in its lady-or-a-vixen ending. "Trent's Trust" (1901) recounts the rags-to-riches success of a young emigrant to California who arrives on the San Francisco wharf "penniless, friendless, and unknown" (IV, 3) and who makes his way by luck and pluck in Horatio Alger fashion. And in "Dick Boyle's Business Card" (1901), a drummer both protects the heroine from Indians and wins her love by promoting his wares as earnestly as he presses his suit.

Dénouement and Death

Many of these *fin de siècle* stories underscore Harte's recurring anxieties about money. His stock gamblers and miners become tropes for the writer in the literary marketplace. His letters of the period are replete with laments on "financial tightness" and his "precarious fortunes" (*L,* 422, 427). His work was still in demand by editors and publishers but, by the mid–1890s, in failing health, he began to take in sail with the inevitable result of reducing his income. "With the ailments I have, I am writing much more slowly each year," he acknowledged (*L,* 495). When Hamlin Garland met him in London, Harte "was affable and polite but looked old and burnt out, his eyes clouded, his skin red and flabby."[35] Still, Harte kept up his membership in the Royal Thames Yacht Club, and he continued to send Anna the monthly draft, although in his "straightened circumstances" he sometimes had to borrow the money.[36] "Every month," he wrote Anna in September 1893, "I have been more or less troubled to get the amount I regularly send you, on account of my health having interfered with the amount of work I can get off."[37] Although his children were grown, they also continued to be a financial drain on him. He was occasionally touched for a loan by his son Frank, who had moved to England in 1893. He "waited until the last moment" to send Anna the draft in March 1895, for example, "in the miserable hope that that miserable Frank would pay me back" the £20 he had borrowed.[38] The irony of this situation was, apparently, lost on the elder Harte. When, in December 1898, he learned that Anna and their daughter Ethel were moving to England and into Frank's home in Caversham, he addressed his son with obvious annoyance: "Of course I can only hope and wish that the arrangements you have thus made may prove perfectly satisfactory to you all, and that in being able to share your house with your mother and sister you may have all the pleasure you have looked forward to."[39] He might still be married to Anna, but he did not have to live with her.

Nor did he hurry to visit her after 22 years. Upon her arrival, he sent her a brief note promising "come up for a day—or at least, *part of day,* very soon."[40] He was as good as his word. Though Harte's debunkers claim he "never saw his wife again" after leaving America in 1878,[41] he in fact visited her several times in Caversham, and his grandson included a late photograph of the family in his edition of Harte's letters. The author obliquely alluded to his reunion with Anna in "The Reincarnation of Smith" (1901), the story of a fellow who, like Hawthorne's Wakefield, abandons his wife only to meet her again years later. To be sure, the Hartes' relations were strained, especially after Anna insisted that her husband pay for music lessons in Paris for Ethel. He would be "quite content," he at length conceded, if these lessons "give her the knowledge and the reputation which she thinks will be valuable to her hereafter." But he cautioned Anna "to keep your promise to keep your expenses within the limits we spoke of."[42]

Unfortunately, her demands on his waning income only increased. Harte learned from a "wretched batch of lying, begging letters" Anna forwarded to him in September 1901 that she routinely diverted part of her monthly allowance to their son Griswold, a ne'er-do-well hack writer, living in New York. He vented frustrations that had been building for years in a remarkable letter which has never before been cited in print. Griswold's appeals for money "are utterly unconvincing," he wrote her. "If you believed . . . that it was your mission to sacrifice yourself and others" for him,

you would never have left America, where, with the money I sent you, you could have easily taken Wodie [Griswold] into your home and looked after him—instead of now expecting the father of over *sixty years,* in his old old age to support a son of *nearly forty!* You would not have wished to add a dubious grandchild to my decreasing income and increasing years. . . .

If you were a rich woman and able to support yourself—or had a husband who was not obliged to work unceasingly, without help from any of his family, even in his old age, you might indulge in such folly. If you had anything out of the $60,000 I have sent you in the last twenty-four years, you might do it. But you are still in debt, after spending that money. . . .

For the last 7 or 8 years I have been warning you of my decreasing income, and my ill health. A month[']s illness would stop your income, three months incapacity for work would be more apt to make *me* a subject for charity and the hospital than it would Wodie.

When you came to England, without my knowledge or consent, I was told by Frank that you expected in that way to reduce your expenses by living with him, and *that* I conceived to have been his reason for advising you to such a rash and expensive step. . . . But [those] expectations have not been realized. You find it necessary for Ethel to study in Paris, and although I finally consented to it, I must tell you frankly, now, that I could not afford it, and had to get money advanced on my work to do it—and am by no means certain that it ever was a necessity! And now, I gather from Frank[']s letters that his plan of making a home for you in his home, and so dividing the expenses is, for some strange reason or other no longer possible. . . .

But I have told you all this before, and am heart-sick with repeating it. It is only when you now calmly prefer "a friend" for the maintainance of a man like Wodie and his child that I do it. You told him that "I had reduced your income"! This is hardly the way to express *my* diminished income. . . . [43]

Griswold died in his house in Brooklyn, apparently by his own hand, three months later.

However callous this letter to Anna may seem in retrospect, Harte's fears for his health were prescient. He was diagnosed with throat cancer early in 1902, and he died a few hours after suffering a hemorrhage while at his writing desk in Mme. Van de Velde's home in Surrey on May 5. Van de Velde paid for his gravestone. She was, in a sense, still providing him with a home. Characteristically, Harte willed his modest estate—barely £360 and all future royalties—to his wife.

Afterword

At his death, Bret Harte was mourned by his American friends largely for what he had failed to accomplish, as a writer whose early promise had been nipped in the bud. Thomas Bailey Aldrich, for example, was saddened by the news of his death "tho' I saw nothing of him and heard nothing of him these last twenty years or more. I dropped reading him when I found that he was not going to add anything to those first eight or ten fine stories of his. What a hit they made!" (*LLWDH* II, 157). Though Henry Adams extolled Harte as one of "the most brilliant men of my time,"[1] the *Bookman* compared his death to "a rustle in the news-papers as of old love-letters and ancient flowers,"[2] and the *Nation* protested that during his long residence abroad he did "not appear to have received a new impression, or made a new observation."[3] The owners of the reincarnated *Overland Monthly* issued a special Harte memorial number in September 1902 and reprinted some of his early poems and stories over the next several months; the implicit assumption was that he had written nothing after leaving California worthy of his reputation. In England, however, Harte was remembered as an earnest and consummate professional. Pemberton wrote privately that Harte's death was "a terrible blow to me. I knew that he was ill but had not realised the gravity of his malady. To the last we were in close corre-spondence concerning a play we were writing together. We were very intimate friends, and I loved him dearly."[4] The *Spectator* averred, with pardonable hyperbole, that he had "probably exerted a greater influ-ence on English literature than any other American author."[5] To the young G. K. Chesterton, he was "a genuine humourist."[6] To be sure, Harte did not found a school of disciples—he mined a pocket, not a lead. But he did inspire a host of imitators, including John Hay in "Pike County Ballads," Constance Fenimore Woolson in "The Lady of Little Fishing," Augustin Daly in the play *Horizon,* Romulo Gallegos in *Doña Bárbara,* Rudyard Kipling in "The Bow Flume Cable-Car," Gertrude Atherton in *Los Cerritos,* Damon Runyon in *Little Miss Marker,* and the pseudonymous author of such stories as "The Pet of Sandy's Bar" and "The Ghosts of the Old Adobe" in the *San Francisco Chronicle.*

Unfortunately, Harte's fears for his family when he was no longer able to provide for them were also realized. Anna and Ethel lived in dire poverty in England for three years until several British authors, among them Conan Doyle and George Meredith, subscribed to a fund to benefit them. His daughter Jessamy, who worked for a time as a cabaret singer, was incarcerated in the early 1920s in the St. Lawrence State Hospital for the Insane in New York. His grandson Richard, an aspiring writer, committed suicide. By the mid–1920s, some journalists referred casually to the self-inflicted "tragedy" of the Hartes, a curse that afflicted the "strangely mixed and strongly marked blood strains" of the clan (Barnett, 235, 250). Like strapped aristocrats squabbling over the family jewels, Harte's heirs also fiercely defended their economic interest in his legacy, negotiating the sale of dramatic rights to his stories to film studios, threatening Houghton Mifflin with a lawsuit in a copyright dispute in 1927, and extorting unreasonable reprint fees from publishers. In 1926, after the *San Francisco Examiner* reprinted some "lost" material Harte wrote for the *Northern Californian* between 1857 and 1860, his grandson Geoffrey contacted Houghton Mifflin to inquire whether he could "obtain payment for the authorization to republish these poems and prose which have just been found, since they seem to be valued at such a high premium."[7] Moreover, like Julian Hawthorne, who sold his father's manuscripts and mementos piecemeal to collectors in the 1880s, Geoffrey Bret Harte (as he signed his name) sold the letters, more than 400 in all, which his grandfather had written to the family over the years. He published the more benign ones in his edition of *The Letters of Bret Harte* (1926). (He apparently did not destroy any of the correspondence, except perhaps the letter in which Harte described his living arrangements in the Van de Velde home after the Count's death, because these holograph manuscripts were valuable commodities on the collectibles market.)

By the time his life had become the stuff of legend, "Bret Harte country" had also been thoroughly surveyed and mapped by the California tourism industry. During his visit to San Francisco in 1889, Kipling was told by Bailey Millard of the *San Francisco Chronicle* that "Bret Harte claims California, but California don't claim Bret Harte." Millard "could not understand," Kipling observed, "that to the outside world the city was worth a great deal less than the man."[8] At Harte's death, however, he had been rediscovered—or, perhaps, reinvented— as a pioneer booster, a sort of Chum Frink of the gold fields, by Californians eager to exploit his persistent popularity. The earliest travelogues through the heart of "Harte's country" were printed around the turn of the century in such western promotional magazines as *Land of Sunshine,* and Tuolumne and Calaveras Counties became popular tourist destinations a generation later with the advent of the touring car and the construction of Highway 49 through the region. "Bret Harte country" was the Disneyland of the 1920s, a proto-amusement park for the working and middle classes, and articles with such self-explanatory titles as "Trailing Bret Harte by Motor" and "Motoring Through the Land of Bret Harte and Mark Twain" appeared in *Sunset* and the automobile section of the *San Francisco Examiner.*[9] In the 1920s and 1930s, the lure of "Bret Harte country" was repeatedly under-scored in guidebooks and other publications, such as *Rider's California,* the *California Journal of Development, Motor Land, Touring Topics,* and *Westways,* with essays specifying various sites/sights associated with Harte's life and stories. As early as 1923, a monument to Harte—accessible almost exclusively by auto—was erected on Mount Diablo, and by 1926 a plaque had been hung on the wall of the rustic cabin in Second Garrotte, California, where the originals of Tennessee and his Partner had lived, asserting that Harte had actually lived there with the two men.[10] "Of all the Californias that men have invented for their delight or their profit," the travel writer Mildred Adams wrote in 1930, "Bret Harte's is the most charming."[11] So pervasive was the appeal of this mythical land that in 1927, according to *Time,* Joseph Stalin established a gold trust to encourage mass migration to Siberia "after reading Bret Harte's novels about the California Gold Rush.[12]

Harte's fame was colored—or, more accurately, his name was black-ened—by the invective Twain heaped on it in the autobiographical dictation first published in 1940 in *Mark Twain in Eruption.* Harte was "one of the unpleasantest men I have ever known," he insisted. "He hadn't a sincere fiber in him. I think he was incapable of emotion, for I think he had nothing to feel with. I think his heart was merely a pump and had no other function. . . . He was bad, distinctly bad; he had no feeling, and he had no conscience. . . . I think the sense of shame was left out of Harte's constitution. . . . The higher passions were left out of Harte; what he knew about them he got from books." He was also "mean," "base," and "treacherous," a man "kept, at dif-ferent times, by a couple of women" (*MTE,* 264, 265, 272, 281, 282, 286). Of course, Twain did not need to rake muck. The truth, while less sensational, is sad enough. Bernard DeVoto also dismissed Harte in *Mark Twain's America* with the contemptuous sneer of an academic *apparatchik*: he was "a literary charlatan whose tales have greatly pleased the second-rate."[13] Unfortunately, the label stuck. DeVoto's comment has recently been quoted approvingly in the *San Francisco Review of Books*.[14] If Twain and DeVoto impeached Harte's character, Brooks and Warren administered the coup de grace to his critical reputation in the first edition of *Understanding Fiction* in 1943. Such stories as "Tennessee's Partner" seemed to epitomize all that was reprehensible to the New Critics: stilted language, incoherent symbolism, unmotivated behavior, confused and sentimental plot. Roy R. Male complained in *Types of Short Fiction* that the tone of "The Luck of Roaring Camp" is "uneven, insecure, and facile," that in it Harte "strains for effect," [15] a capital crime in the aesthetics of formalism. By rights, such pointed attacks on the faint and false Harte should have buried forever the buckskin dandy of the slick illustrated weeklies.

Like the monster in the Saturday matinee, however, he never seems to die for long. Thirty years after assailing "Tennessee's Partner" in *Understanding Fiction,* Brooks and Warren, with R. W. B. Lewis, reprinted it, albeit without comment, in *American Literature: The Makers and the Making*. Almost every American literature anthology available today includes a chestnut or two by Harte. No fewer than 34 of his titles are now in press, as well as a reprint of the 20-volume 1903 library edition of his works, a reprint of his grandson's selection of his letters, and 10 paperback collections of his stories suitable for classroom adoption. His holograph letters sell for upwards to $750 apiece, and the nine-page manuscript of his semiautobiographical essay "How I Went to the Mines" was recently listed for $25,000.[16] His name adorns schools and saloons throughout northern California. His best stories are as durable, if not as stylish, as denim pants. In the end, they lack everything but an audience.

Notes on the References and Acknowledgments

Abbreviations

I have cited throughout the notes and parenthetically within the text, by volume and page numbers alone, the 25-volume edition of *The Works of Bret Harte* (New York: Collier, 1906). The following abbreviations are used to refer to other primary and secondary works:

AS	Bret Harte and Mark Twain, *"Ah Sin": A Dramatic Work,* ed. Frederick Anderson (San Francisco: Book Club of California, 1961).
Barnett	Linda Diz Barnett, *Bret Harte: A Reference Guide* (Boston: G. K. Hall, 1980).
BHC	*Bret Harte's California,* ed. Gary Scharnhorst (Albuquerque: University of New Mexico Press, 1990).
Booth 1944	Bradford A. Booth, "Unpublished Letters of Bret Harte," *American Literature,* 16 (May 1944), 131–42.
Booth 1948	——— "Bret Harte Goes East: Some Unpublished Letters," *American Literature,* 19 (January 1948), 318–35.
Booth 1954	——— "Mark Twain's Comments on Bret Harte's Stories," *American Literature,* 25 (January 1954), 492–95.
Daly	Joseph F. Daly, *The Life of Augustin Daly* (New York: Macmillan, 1917).
Dam	Henry J. W. Dam, "A Morning with Bret Harte," *McClure's,* 4 (December 1894), 38–50.
Duckett 1953	Margaret Duckett, "Bret Harte's Portrayal of Half-Breeds," *American Literature,* 25 (May 1953), 193–12
Duckett 1957	———, "Plain Language from Bret Harte," *Nineteenth Century Fiction,* 11 (March 1957), 241–60.
Duckett 1964	———, *Mark Twain and Bret Harte* (Norman: University of Oklahoma Press, 1964).
Felheim	Marvin Felheim, *The Theatre of Augustin Daly* (Cambridge: Harvard University Press, 1956).
GC	*Gabriel Conroy* (Boston and New York: Houghton Mifflin, 1896). 2 vols.
Harrison	Joseph B. Harrison, *Bret Harte: Representative Selections* (New York: American Book Co., 1941).

Haskell   Mabel Percy Haskell, "Bret Harte in London," *San Francisco Examiner,* 12 February 1893, 17:4–5.

Howe   M. A. DeWolfe Howe, *Memories of a Hostess* (Boston: Atlantic Monthly Press, 1922).

Kozlay   *Stories and Poems and Other Uncollected Writings,* ed. Charles M. Kozlay (Boston and New York: Houghton Mifflin, 1914).

L   *The Letters of Bret Harte,* ed. Geoffrey Bret Harte (Boston and New York: Houghton Mifflin, 1926).

LFA   W. D. Howells, *Literary Friends and Acquaintance* (New York: Harper & Brothers, 1900).

LLWDH   *Life in Letters of William Dean Howells,* ed. Mildred Howells (Garden City, N.Y.: Doubleday, 1928). 2 vols.

M&M   Brenda Murphy and George Monteiro, "The Unpublished Letters of Bret Harte to John Hay," *American Literary Realism,* 12 (Spring 1979), 77–110.

MTE   *Mark Twain in Eruption,* ed. Bernard DeVoto (New York and London: Harper & Brothers, 1940).

MT–HL   *Mark Twain–Howells Letters,* ed. Henry Nash Smith and William M. Gibson (Cambridge: Belknap, 1960). 2 vols.

MTL   *Mark Twain's Letters,* ed. Edgar Marquess Branch et al. (Berkeley, Los Angeles, and London: University of California Press, 1988, 1990). 2 vols.

Outcasts   Bret Harte, *The Outcasts of Poker Flat and Other Tales* (New York: Signet, 1961).

Pemberton   T. Edgar Pemberton, *The Life of Bret Harte* (London: Pearson, 1903).

Quinn   Arthur Hobson Quinn, *American Fiction: An Historical and Critical Survey* (New York and London: Appleton–Century, 1936).

"Rise"   Bret Harte, "The Rise of the 'Short Story,'" *Cornhill,* NS 7 (July 1899), 1–8.

Rosenthal   Lewis Rosenthal, "Bret Harte in Germany," *Critic,* 21 February 1885, 85.

Stewart   George R. Stewart, Jr., *Bret Harte: Argonaut and Exile* (Boston and New York: Houghton Mifflin, 1931).

Williams   Stanley T. Williams, *The Spanish Background of American Literature* (New Haven, Conn.: Yale University Press, 1955). 2 vol.

Young   James Harvey Young, "Anna Dickinson, Mark Twain, and Bret Harte," *Pennsylvania Magazine of History and Biography,* 76 (January 1952), 39–46.

Manuscript Locations

The following abbreviations are used in the notes to specify the locations of manuscript material:

Bancroft	Bancroft Library, University of California, Berkeley, Calif.
Cornell	Olin Library, Cornell University, Ithaca, N.Y.
Folger	Folger Shakespeare Library, Washington, D.C.
Hayes	Rutherford B. Hayes Presidential Center, Fremont, Ohio.
H–B	Hampden–Booth Theatre Library, New York, N.Y.
Houghton	Houghton Library, Harvard University, Cambridge, Mass.
Huntington	Huntington Library, San Marino, Calif.
Indiana	Lilly Library, Indiana University, Bloomington, Ind.
Knox	Knox College Library, Galesburg, Ill.
LC	Manuscript Division, Library of Congress, Washington, D.C.
MHNP	Morristown Historical National Park, Morristown, N.J.
MHS	Massachusetts Historical Society, Boston, Mass.
MiHS	Minnesota Historical Society, St. Paul, Minn.
Princeton	Princeton University Library, Princeton, N.J.
SFPL	San Francisco Public Library, San Francisco, Calif.
UCLA	Research Library, University of California at Los Angeles, Los Angeles, Calif.
UVa	Alderman Library, University of Virginia, Charlottesville, Va.
Wesleyan	Olin Memorial Library, Wesleyan University, Middletown, Conn.
Yale	Beinecke Library, Yale University, New Haven, Conn.

Notes and References

Preface

1. *St. Louis Republic,* 9 December 1900, Sunday magazine, 1.
2. *New York Herald,* 29 August 1876, 5:4.
3. *Saturday Review of Literature,* 17 April 1926, 717.
4. *Mark Twain's Letters,* 3 vols., ed. A. B. Paine (New York and London: Harper & Bros., 1917), I, 182–83.

Chapter One

1. Harte to Rossiter Johnson, 11 May 1874 (Houghton). Basically the same statement appears in Harte's letter to E. C. Stedman, 16 September 1887 (UVa).
2. *Journal of the West,* 19 (January 1980), 9.
3. Harte to Anna Harte, 4 March 1879 (UCLA).
4. Harte to Anna Harte, 15 September 1885 (Bancroft).
5. Henry Childs Merwin, *The Life of Bret Harte* (Boston and New York: Houghton Mifflin, 1911), 16; Howe, 238.
6. Diary, 31 December 1857 (Bancroft). Also cited in Stewart, 68–69.
7. Harte to George Baintree, 1 November 1888 (Bancroft).
8. Diary, 1 December 1857 (Bancroft).
9. *Golden Era,* 10 January 1857, 2.
10. *California Historical Society Quarterly,* 45 (June 1966), 108.
11. *Souvenirs of My Time* (Boston: D. Lothrop & Co., 1887), 204–205.
12. *Boston Transcript,* 22 January 1863, 1:2; and *Littell's Living Age,* 21 February 1863, 382; Stewart, 114, 116.
13. T. S. King to J. T. Fields, 31 January 1862 (Huntington).
14. *Boston Transcript,* 7 November 1862, 2:3.
15. *Boston Traveller Supplement,* 26 September 1863, 1:5.
16. Williams, 211; James C. Austin, *Fields of the Atlantic Monthly* (San Marino, Calif.: Huntington Library, 1953), 369.
17. Frémont, "What Makes Literary Success?" *Ladies' Home Journal,* NS 9 (February 1892), 18.
18. H[arris] E[lwood] S[tarr], "King, Thomas Starr," *DAB* (1933), X, 403–405.
19. Robert Glass Cleland, *From Wilderness to Empire* (New York: Knopf, 1944), 303.
20. *Western American Literature,* 8 (Fall 1973), 142.
21. *San Francisco Daily Dramatic Chronicle,* 11 January 1866, 2:2.

22. *New York Evening Post,* 12 December 1865, 1:1–2; *New York Home Journal,* 30 December 1865.

23. Quoted in *San Francisco Daily Dramatic Chronicle,* 31 January 1866, 2:1.

24. Quoted in *San Francisco Bulletin,* 6 January 1866, 1:2–3.

25. *San Francisco Bulletin,* 21 December 1865, 5:6.

26. Quoted in *San Francisco Bulletin,* 6 January 1866, 1:1. For the record, other unlisted reviews of *Outcroppings* appeared in the *Springfield Republican,* 22 November 1865, 1:1; *Sacramento Union,* 20 December 1865, 3:3; and *Athenaeum,* 3 March 1866, 299.

27. *New York Times,* 15 February 1866, 8:3–5. See also *Sacramento Union,* 8 December 1865, 3:3–4; 15 December 1865, 3:3; and 22 December 1865, 3:4; Stewart, 134.

28. *San Francisco Examiner,* 8 January 1866, 3:1.

29. *North American Review,* 102 (April 1866), 588.

30. *Concerning "Condensed Novels"* (Palo Alto, Calif.: Stanford University Press, 1929), xix; Harte to S. W. Bush, 22 November 1867 (MHS).

31. *San Francisco Alta California,* 10 November 1867, 2:2; *San Francisco Evening Bulletin,* 9 November 1867, 1:1.

32. *Atlantic Monthly,* 21 (January 1868), 128.

33. Harte to J. T. Fields, 30 October 1868 (Huntington).

34. Harte to J. R. Osgood, 1 January 1871 (Huntington–Kozlay bibliography).

35. *San Francisco Chronicle,* 2 July 1882, 6:3.

36. *San Francisco Bulletin,* 11 January 1868, 1:7. See also *San Francisco Bulletin,* 21 December 1867, 1:1-2; *San Francisco Daily Drmatic Chronicle,* 30 December 1867, 2:2; and Barnett, 2–4.

37. *San Francisco Bulletin,* 6 June 1867, 1:4–5.

38. *Springfield Republican,* 26 September 1866, 2:2. The poem also appeared in the *Portland Transcript,* 8 September 1866, 164; and in the *St. Louis Daily Missouri Republican,* 7 October 1866, 1:3.

39. *New York Tribune,* 30 April 1878, 2:4.

40. Harte to C. H. Webb, 18 October 1866 (Bancroft).

41. Harte to Warren Sawyer, 18 December 1866 (MHS).

42. *Springfield Republican,* 16 January 1867, 4:3.

43. *Springfield Republican,* 22 May 1867, 1:6.

44. *Springfield Republican,* 25 April 1870, 2:2.

Chapter Two

1. Harte to J. L. VerMehr, 2 February 1868 (Bancroft).

2. Harte to Henry Bellows, 9 April 1869 (MHS).

3. *American Literature,* 22 (November 1950), 262.

4. *New York Sun,* 20 July 1879, 2:7. Harte hotly disputed Roman's version of the story in a private letter to his wife (*L,* 152–53).

5. *Springfield Republican,* 9 September 1868, 2:2; 12 September 1868, 6:1–3; and 30 September 1868, 2:2. The story was also reprinted in the *Portland Transcript,* 31 October 1868, pp. 241–42.

6. *The Letters of George Meredith,* ed. C. L. Cline (Oxford: Charendon, 1970), I, 462.

7. Harte to J. T. Fields, 30 October 1868 (Huntington).

8. *Soundings,* 57 (Summer 1974), 198.

9. *Nineteenth Century Fiction,* 22 (December 1967), 275.

10. "Introduction" to *The Outcasts of Poker Flat and Other Tales* (New York: Signet, 1961), viii.

11. See Harte's poem "Dickens in Camp" (VIII, 209–10), which alludes explicitly to *The Old Curiosity Shop.* On Dickens's influence on Harte, see also Stewart, 22, 99, 164; Lucy Lockwood Hazard, *The Frontier in American Literature* (New York: Crowell, 1927), 196–97; and *Canadian Review of American Studies,* 2 (Fall 1971), 89–101.

12. "General Introduction" to *The Writings of Bret Harte* (Boston and New York: Houghton Mifflin, 1906), xviii.

13. *American Literary Realism,* 23 (Winter 1991), 56.

14. Ina Coolbrith to Charles Warren Stoddard, 9 January 1869 (Huntington).

15. "Introduction" to *The Great Modern American Stories* (New York: Boni and Liveright, 1920), xiii.

16. *Heroines of Fiction* (New York and London: Harper & Brothers, 1901), II, 228.

17. *Understanding Fiction* (New York: Appleton–Century–Crofts, 1959), 181, 184.

18. *Arizona Quarterly,* 36 (Autumn 1980), 213–14.

19. *Studies in Short Fiction,* 17 (Spring 1980), 115.

20. *South Dakota Review,* 15 (Spring 1977), 116–17.

21. *The Scarlet Letter,* ed. Sculley Bradley *et al.* (New York: Norton, 1978), 183–84.

22. *Overland Monthly,* 4 (January 1870), 100–101.

23. *Bret Harte: Literary Critic* (Bowling Green, Ohio: Popular Press, 1979), 88, 63.

24. *Strive and Succeed* (New York: New York Book Co., 1909), 53; *Tom the Bootblack* (New York: Hurst, n.d.), 213; *The Young Miner* (Chicago: Donahue, n.d.), 57.

25. Edgar M. Kahn, *Bret Harte in California* (San Francisco: privately printed, 1951), 7.

26. Frank Luther Mott, *A History of American Magazines 1865–1885* (Cambridge: Harvard University Press, 1938), 405.

27. Quoted in Robert L. Fulton, "Bret Harte and Truthful James," *Overland Monthly*, 67 (August 1915), 94.

28. Harte to J. H. Carmany, 8 June 1869 (Bancroft); *L*, 8.

29. Ella Sterling Cummins, *The Story of the Files* (San Francisco: Cooperative Printing Co., 1893), 146.

30. S. L. Conant to Harte, 15 December 1870 (LC).

31. Harte to Parke Godwin, 9 July 1870 (UVa).

32. Harte to F. P. Church, 18 October 1870 (Bancroft).

33. Barnett, 5–14; *Springfield Republican*, 25 April 1870, 2:1–2. Howells would later estimate sales of this volume during its first six months in press at only 3,500 copies (*LFA*, 301).

34. Stewart, 183–84; *San Francisco Alta California*, 17 August 1870, 1:1; and 4 October 1870, 1:3.

35. *San Francisco Alta California*, 8 January 1871, 2:2.

36. *San Francisco Alta California*, 2 February 1871, 2:1.

Chapter Three

1. *Springfield Republican*, 20 March 1871, 2:4. "In the Mission Garden" appeared in *Harper's Weekly* for 15 April 1871.

2. Frank Luther Mott, *A History of American Magazines 1850–1865* (Cambridge: Harvard University Press, 1938), 505.

3. Harte to J. R. Osgood, 6 March 1871 (Bancroft); *L*, 12.

4. Harte to J. R. Osgood, 1 April 1871 (Houghton).

5. Harte to J. R. Osgood, 4 April 1871 (UVa).

6. *New York Tribune*, 11 March 1871, 6:1.

7. Clara Barrus, *Whitman and Burroughs, Comrades* (Boston: Houghton Mifflin, 1931), 64.

8. *Fun*, 21 October 1871, 180.

9. *If Not Literature: Letters of Elinor Mead Howells*, ed. Ginette de B. Merrill and George Arms (Columbus: Ohio State University Press, 1988), 146.

10. *New York Evening Post*, 27 February 1872, 1:1.

11. *Henry James Letters*, ed. Leon Edel (Cambridge: Belknap, 1974), I, 269–70.

12. Harte to John Spencer Clark, 27 September 1872 (UVa).

13. *New York Times Saturday Review of Books and Art*, 24 May 1902, 350.

14. *San Francisco Chronicle*, 15 December 1872, 1:1.

15. *London Times*, 22 June 1880, 12:1.

16. *The Lectures of Bret Harte*, ed. Charles Meeker Kozlay (London: privately printed, 1909), 7.

17. Harte to Rudolf Schneider, 21 December 1879 (UVa).

18. Harte to J. T. Fields, 18 December 1871 (Huntington).

19. Harte to Hiram Corson, 25 April 1874 (Cornell).

20. Harte to J. R. Osgood, 6 October 1875 (UVa).

21. *San Francisco Alta California,* 23 February 1875, 2:1.

22. Harte to Jenny Gilder, 18 November 1873 (UVa).

23. Harte to Anna Harte, n.d. [ca. 1874] (UVa).

24. Harte to W. D. Howells, 2 September 1874 (Hayes).

25. Harte to Mary E. W. Sherwood, 31 October 1875 (Bancroft).

26. Harte to Bessie Ward, 19 September 1874 (UVa).

27. Harte to Elisha Bliss, 7 March 1875 (Huntington).

28. Harte to Elisha Bliss, 18 January 1875 (MHNP).

29. *New York Times,* 17 January 1875, 5:1.

30. *L,* 51; Box 1, Morse Collection (UCLA).

31. Harte to Elisha Bliss, 23 February 1875 (UVa).

32. Harte to J. R. Osgood, 6 October 1875 (UVa).

33. *Saturday Review,* 24 June 1876, 817.

34. "Lawrence Barrett: a wealth of wild roses" (MS in private collection of V. B. Price), 9.

35. *London Times,* 21 June 1876, 5:6.

36. *Illustrated London News,* 17 June 1876, 594.

37. *Athenaeum,* 3 June 1876, 762.

38. *Springfield Republican,* 12 July 1876, 5:1.

39. *Atlantic Monthly,* 50 (August 1882), 266.

40. *Bret Harte: A Biography* (Boston: Little, Brown, 1966), 171.

41. Stewart, 227; Harte to J. R. Osgood, 3 March 1880 (Bancroft).

42. *Philological Quarterly,* 33 (October 1954), 442–44.

43. Harte to J. R. Osgood, 3 March 1880 (Bancroft).

44. Box 1, Morse Collection (UCLA).

45. Harte to Bessie Ward, 19 September 1874 (UVa).

46. *New York Clipper,* 27 August 1870; *Springfield Republican,* 30 March 1871, 2:4; John Bonner to Augustin Daly, 17 March 1871 (Folger).

47. John Bonner to Augustin Daly, 17 March 1871 (Folger). See also *MT–HL* I, 33.

48. Daly, 171–75. See also Arthur Hobson Quinn, *A History of the American Drama* (New York: Crofts, 1943), I, 109; and Brenda Murphy, *American Realism and American Drama, 1880–1940* (Cambridge: Cambridge University Press, 1987), 51.

49. Harte's letter of agreement with Stuart Robson, 18 March 1875 (H–B).

50. *New York Evening Post,* 4 September 1876, 2:3.

51. Harte to Lawrence Barrett, 22 September 1875 (Knox).

52. Harte's holograph version of the play is located in the Huntington Library.

53. *Chicago Tribune,* 18 July 1876, 2:5–6 and 23 July 1876, 13:3–4.

54. *Chicago Inter-Ocean,* 18 July 1876, 8:5; and 22 July 1876, 2:4.

55. Leonard Grover to A. H. Palmer, 7 August 1876 (H–B).

56. *New York Times,* 29 August 1876, 5:4–5 and 3 September 1876, 7:2.

57. *MTL,* II, 33; *New York Tribune,* 29 August 1876, 5:1.

58. *New York Herald,* 29 August 1876, 5:4.

59. *New York Evening Post,* 29 August 1876, 2:4 and 30 August 1876, 2:4; *New York Commercial Advertiser,* 29 August 1876, 1:3. See also the *New York World,* 29 August 1876, 5:2; *Appleton's Journal,* NS 1 (October 1876), 380; *Hartford Courant,* 20 October 1876, 1:8; *Boston Transcript,* 7 November 1876, 5:2; *Baltimore American,* 10 October 1876, 5:8; and *Galaxy,* 22 (November 1876), 721–22.

60. *Library Table,* 13 (September 1877), 174.

61. *New York World,* 3 September 1876, 6:3; Harte to Wheeler, 3 September 1876 (UVa).

62. *New York Times,* 2 September 1876, 5:2.

63. *New York Herald,* 3 September 1876, 5:4.

64. *Hartford Courant,* 5 September 1876, 1:8.

65. *New York Tribune,* 4 September 1876, 4:5.

66. *New York Evening Post,* 4 September 1876, 2:3.

67. *New York Sun,* 7 September 1876, 2:4; *New York Commercial Advertiser,* 9 September 1876, 2:3.

68. *New York World,* 10 September 1876, 4:6.

69. *New York Sun,* 14 September 1876, 2:6. This letter was quoted at length in the *Boston Transcript* the next day (4:1–2).

70. Quoted in *New York World,* 15 September 1876, 4:4–5.

71. *New York Sun,* 15 September 1876, 2:4.

72. *New York World,* 17 September 1876, 4:1.

73. *New York Daily Graphic,* 22 September 1876, p. 568; *New York Evening Mail,* 22 September 1876, 2:3–4.

74. *New York World,* 23 September 1876, 4:5. When the script appeared as a book the following spring, the *New York World* added that "we should be very much afraid after all that has happened to be obliged" to review the play again (23 April 1877, 2:2).

75. *New York Clipper,* 23 September 1876, p. 202.

76. *Nation,* 28 September 1876, p. 200.

77. Harte to J. R. Osgood, 3 October 1878 (Yale).

78. C. D. Warner to C. H. Webb, 27 October 1876 (Bancroft).

79. *Atlantic Monthly,* 39 (January 1877), 103. Anna Dickinson also believed the "markedly personal" tone of the review in the *New York Times* was the result of jealousy (Young, 45–46).

80. *St. Louis Globe–Democrat,* 21 January 1877, 3:4.

81. *San Francisco Examiner,* 1 May 1892, 10:2.

82. Stuart Robson to Harte, 6 October 1876 (Bancroft).

83. *San Francisco Alta California,* 29 September 1878, 2:2. See also Glen Loney's introduction to *California Gold-Rush Plays* (New York: Performing Arts Journal Publications, 1983), 19.

84. *American Literary Realism,* 21 (Fall 1988), 61.

85. *AS,* xiii. The original promptbook of the play is located in the Alderman Library at UVa. See also the *New York Tribune,* 1 August 1877, 5:1.

86. Harte to Donn Piatt, 20 August 1877 (Hayes).

87. *Atlantic Monthly,* 78 (November 1896), 676–67.

88. *San Francisco Chronicle,* 2 July 1882, 6:3.

89. *Boston Advertiser,* 6 February 1877, 2:4.

90. *New York World,* 29 January 1877, 2:2.

91. Harte to Donn Piatt, 20 August 1877 (Hayes).

92. Harte to M. E. W. Sherwood, 9 March 1878 (UVa).

93. Harte to Anna Harte, n.d. [ca. late September 1877] (Bancroft).

94. *Cincinnati Gazette,* 10 January 1878, 5:4; rpt. *San Francisco Alta California,* 27 January 1878, 1:2.

95. Harte to Anna Harte, 27 December 1878 and 24 September 1893 (Bancroft); Harte to Ethel Harte, 14 September 1889 (UVa).

96. *Literary World,* 1 March 1878, 181.

97. *Chats About Books, Poets and Novelists* (New York: Scribner's, 1883), 297.

98. *Boston Traveller,* 15 May 1878, 4:2.

99. William Copeland to the editors of the *New York Daily Bulletin,* 12 October 1877 (Bancroft).

100. Harte to Homer Lee, 2 April 1878 (UVa).

101. Harte to J. R. Osgood, 9 March 1878 (Bancroft).

102. Harte to Donn Piatt, 20 August 1877 (Hayes).

Chapter Four

1. *San Francisco Chronicle,* 14 September 1873, 6:5.

2. *Literary World,* 8 (June 1877), 12.

3. *Blätter für literarische Unterhaltung,* 15 November 1877, 730.

4. *Jahrbuch für Amerikastudien,* 10 (1965), 219.

5. Harte to J. R. Osgood, 19 July 1878 (Houghton).

6. Harte to H. J. Winser, 1 August 1878 (Bancroft).

7. Harte to Wemyss Reid, 24 May 1879 (Bancroft).

8. *Argonaut,* 9 November 1876, 9.

9. Harte to Anna Harte, 15 September 1901 (UVa).

10. Harte to Anna Harte, 27 December 1878 (Bancroft).

11. Harte to Anna Harte, 14 June 1883 (Bancroft).

12. *Argonaut,* 10 April 1880, 4.

13. *Athenaeum,* 22 March 1879, 375.

14. *Revue de Littérature Comparee,* 54 (April–June 1980), 223.

15. *Markham Review,* 3 (May 1973), 101–105.

16. Harte to the editor of the *Berliner Tageblatt,* 2 January 1879 (Princeton).

17. *Nineteenth-Century,* 8 (August 1880), 338; *Athenaeum,* 13 March 1880, 342.

18. *Athenaeum,* 13 March 1880, 342.

19. *Hartford Courant,* 14 November 1879, 2:2.

20. Harte to Charles A. Dana, 1 October 1879 (MiHS).

21. *L,* 177; *Literary World,* 22 May 1880, 172.

22. Harte to Gertrude Griswold, 10 September 1878 (Huntington).

23. *San Francisco Examiner,* 7 July 1895, 25:2.

24. Harte to Frau Schneider, 11 August 1880 (UVa).

25. *New York Tribune,* 9 March 1881, 6:2.

26. Harte to J. R. Osgood, 10 May 1879 (UVa).

27. Harte to Frau Schneider, 8 May 1887 (UVa).

28. *Bookman,* 39 (March 1914), 46–47.

29. Wemyss Reid, *William Black: Novelist* (New York and London: Harper, 1902), 216, 218.

30. *LFA,* 294. See also Kozlay, 256–65.

31. *The Diaries of Lewis Carroll,* ed. Roger L. Green (New York: Oxford University Press, 1954), II, 387.

32. Harte to Frau Schneider, 14 December 1880 (UVa).

33. *Literary World,* 23 September 1882, 315.

34. Harte to Anna Harte, 14 June 1883 (UVa).

35. *The Education of Henry Adams* (Boston: Houghton Mifflin, 1961), 385.

36. *Critic,* 7 October 1882, 266.

37. *Western American Literature,* 8 (Fall 1973), 95.

38. *Spectator,* 1 September 1883, 1129; *Dial,* 4 (October 1883), 128.

39. Harte to Charles A. Dana, 13 November 1883 (UVa).

40. *Academy,* 16 August 1884, 105.

41. Harte to Anna Harte, 8 February 1883 (Bancroft).

42. Harte to Anna Harte, 14 June 1883 (Bancroft); certificate of satisfaction, Ralph Teets and Joh. Trockmorton vs. Bret Harte (LC).

43. Harte to Anna Harte, 4 August 1883 (Bancroft).

44. Harte to Anna Harte, 10 November 1883 (Bancroft).

45. Harte to Frau Schneider, 1 November 1881 (UVa).

46. Harte to Anna Harte, 15 April 1884 (Bancroft).

47. Harte to Frau Schneider, 6 January 1886 (UVa).

48. Harte to Anna Harte, 7 February 1883 (SFPL).

49. Harte to Anna Harte, 27 December 1884 (Bancroft).

50. Harte to Anna Harte, 15 May 1885 (UVa).

51. Harte to Frau Schneider, 25 May 1885 (UVa).

52. Harte to Frau Schneider, 3 August 1885 (UVa).

53. *Washington Post,* 17 December 1885, 6:1.

54. *Athenaeum,* 31 December 1898, 928.

55. Harte to Anna Harte, 17 September 1889 (Bancroft).

56. Harte to Anna Harte, 4 August 1883 (Bancroft).

57. Harte to Florence Henniker, 30 May 1890 (UVa).

58. Harte to Gertrude Griswold, 18 March 1882 (Huntington).

59. Harte to Frau Schneider, 29 August 1882 (UVa).

60. *L,* 218; *MT–HL* I, 416; Harte to Anna Harte, 7 February 1883 (SFPL).

61. Harte to Anna Harte, 7 February 1883 (SFPL).

62. Harte to Anna Harte, 4 August 1883 (Bancroft).

63. *L,* 355. Harte negotiated an arrangement that would pay him £15 per week as long as Boucicault's play remained on the stage (Harte to Boucicault's heirs, 5 November 1890, LC). Boucicault's version of "The Luck of Roaring Camp" was produced in New York in 1894.

64. Booth 1944, 137–38; *L,* 329; Harte to Anna Harte, 17 September 1889 (Bancroft).

65. Booth 1944, 139; *L,* 352–54, 459; Pemberton, 265. See also Harte's letter to Pemberton, 2 November 1898 (Yale): "I have sometimes thought that *my material* was not the kind from which a popular play could be made."

66. Harte to Mary S. Boyd, 31 January 1895 (UCLA).

67. Harte to T. Edgar Pemberton, 22 May 1895 (Yale).

68. Harte to T. Edgar Pemberton, 11 June 1895 (Yale).

69. Harte to T. Edgar Pemberton, 3 June 1896 (Yale).

70. *Harper's Weekly,* 10 October 1896, 998.

71. *Sue* (London: Greening & Co. Ltd., 1902), passim.

72. *New York Tribune,* 16 September 1896, 7:1. Horatio Alger, Jr., attended a performance of *Sue* at the Museum Theatre in Boston and wrote later that the plot was "faulty" and that he did not "on the whole" consider the play "a success" (Alger to Irving Blake, 3 December and 12 December 1896, Huntington).

73. Harte to T. Edgar Pemberton, 4 October 1896 (Yale).

74. Harte to T. Edgar Pemberton, 5 January 1897 (Yale).

75. Harte to T. Edgar Pemberton, 4 April 1897 (Yale).

76. Harte to T. Edgar Pemberton, 5 December 1900 (Yale).

77. Harte to T. Edgar Pemberton, 4 April 1897 (Yale).

78. Harte to Anna Harte, 29 October 1897 (UCLA).

79. Harte to T. Edgar Pemberton, 12 August 1896 (Yale).

80. Harte to T. Edgar Pemberton, 2 November 1898 (Yale).

81. Pemberton, 263–64; Harte to Hatton, 19 January 1899 (Bancroft).

82. *L,* 246; *New York Times,* 20 January 1884, 10:1–2; Harte to Mary S. Boyd, June 1895 (UCLA).

83. Harte to T. Edgar Pemberton, 2 November 1898 (Yale).

Chapter Five

1. Harte to Anna Harte, 15 September 1885 (Bancroft).

2. Harte to Frau Schneider, 25 May 1885 (UVa).

3. Harte to Frau Schneider, 6 January 1886 (UVa).

4. Harte to Anna Harte, 23 August 1893 (Wesleyan).

5. Harte to Florence Henniker, 23 April 1890 (UVa).

6. *Dial,* 6 (November 1885), 124.

7. Harte to Florence Henniker, 23 April 1890 (UVa).

8. Harte to Florence Henniker, 19 February 1890 (UVa).

9. *Boston Transcript,* 3 February 1887, 6:4–5.

10. *L,* 427; Stewart, 322, 325; Harte to Gertrude Griswold, 1 March 1880 (Huntington). See also I, 190; V, 3; and *GC* I, 14.

11. *Critic,* 16 April 1898, 265.

12. *Southern Review,* 18 (July 1875), 96.

13. *Overland Monthly,* NS 9 (January 1887), 111.

14. *New York Times Saturday Review of Books and Art,* 17 May 1902, 334. This review quotes verbatim, albeit without attribution, from Harte's "Miss Peggy's Protégées" (IX, 283).

15. *Literary World,* 8 April 1882, 116.

16. *Complete Works of Oscar Wilde* (Garden City, N.Y.: Doubleday, Page & Co., 1923), XII, 136–37.

17. *Tennessee Studies in Literature,* 4 (1959), 115.

18. *Boston Transcript,* 4 November 1887, 6:5.

19. *London Times,* 9 November 1887, 4:5.

20. *Independent,* 6 October 1887, 1269.

21. *New York Tribune,* 10 July 1887, 10:3.

22. Harte to Anna Harte, 22 June 1892 (UVa).

23. *Adventures of a Novelist* (New York: Liveright, 1932), 181. See also *MTE,* 264–65.

24. *Boston Transcript,* 18 December 1895, 10:4.

25. *Western American Literature,* 8 (Fall 1973), 148.

26. *San Francisco Chronicle,* 5 February 1893, 9:2.

27. Harte to Richard Watson Gilder, 29 June 1900 (MNHP).

28. *New York Times,* 6 October 1895, 27:5.

29. *The Unwritten War* (New York: Knopf, 1973), 328.

30. Harte to Mary Boyd, 5 November 1894 (UCLA).

31. *San Francisco Examiner,* 1 December 1895, 33:5.

32. Harte alludes here, however obliquely, to the widespread belief at the time that Mark Twain had written a doggerel poem in imitation of Harte

entitled "Three Aces" in 1870 under the pseudonym *Carl Byng*. The poet and the highwayman in Harte's story share the same peculiar surname, and their first names are etymologically related (the German Carl or Karl = the French Charles). Thus Harte seems to imply that, like Martinez, Mark Twain (even these names share six letters in sequence) was no better than a thief hiding behind an alias.

33. *Mark Twain Journal*, 14 (Winter 1967–68), 6.
34. *Nation*, 26 July 1894, 68.
35. *Hamlin Garland's Diaries*, ed. Donald Pizer (San Marino, Calif.: Huntington Library, 1968), 143.
36. Harte to Francis King Harte, 14 December 1898 (UVa).
37. Harte to Anna Harte, 24 September 1893 (Bancroft).
38. Harte to Anna Harte, 30 March 1895 (SFPL).
39. Harte to Francis King Harte, 14 December 1898 (UVa).
40. Harte to Anna Harte, n.d. [ca. early January 1899?] (UCLA).
41. *Norton Anthology of American Literature*, ed. Ronald Gottesman et al. (New York and London: Norton, 1979), II, 285.
42. Harte to Anna Harte, 1 December 1900 (UVa).
43. Harte to Anna Harte, 15 September 1901 (UVa).

Afterword

1. *Letters of Henry Adams 1892–1918*, ed. Worthington Chauncey Ford (Boston and New York: Houghton Mifflin, 1938), 391.
2. *Bookman*, 15 (July 1902), 466–67.
3. *Nation*, 26 June 1902, 502.
4. T. Edgar Pemberton to William Winter, 24 June 1902 (Indiana).
5. *Spectator*, 10 May 1902, 715.
6. *Varied Types* (New York: Dodd, Mead, 1903), 179.
7. Geoffrey Bret Harte to Mr. Pratt, 21 June 1926 (Houghton).
8. *Kipling in California*, ed. Thomas Pinney (Berkeley: Bancroft Library, 1989), 45.
9. Peter B. Kyne, "Trailing Bret Harte by Motor," *Sunset*, 31 (July 1913), 97–107; Barnett, 229.
10. Barnett, 240; George King, "The Sierran Home of Bret Harte," *Touring Topics*, 18 (June 1926), 29.
11. *New York Times Magazine*, 31 August 1930, 12–13.
12. *Time*, 15 May 1964, 107–108.
13. *Mark Twain's America* (Boston: Little, Brown, 1932), 164.
14. *San Francisco Review of Books*, Fall 1990, 21.
15. *Types of Short Fiction* (Belmont, Calif.: Wadsworth, 1962), 304.
16. Kenneth W. Rendell, Inc., catalogue 193 (1990), 17; Heritage Book Shop, Inc., catalogue 178 [1990], 15.

Selected Bibliography

PRIMARY SOURCES

Collected Editions

The Works of Bret Harte. Argonaut Edition. New York: P. F. Collier & Son, 1906. 25 vols.
The Writings of Bret Harte. Standard Library Edition. Boston and New York: Houghton Mifflin, 1896–1904. 20 vols.

First Editions

Condensed Novels and Other Papers. New York: Carleton, 1867.
The Lost Galleon and Other Tales. San Francisco: Towne & Bacon, 1867.
The Luck of Roaring Camp and Other Sketches. Boston: Fields, Osgood, 1870.
Poems. Boston: Fields, Osgood, 1871.
Mrs. Skagg's Husbands and Other Sketches. Boston: Osgood, 1873.
Echoes of the Foot-Hills. Boston: Osgood, 1875.
Tales of the Argonauts and Other Sketches. Boston: Osgood, 1875.
Gabriel Conroy. Hartford: American Publishing Co., 1876.
Two Men of Sandy Bar. Boston: Osgood, 1876.
Thankful Blossom: A Romance of the Jerseys. Boston: Osgood, 1877.
The Story of a Mine. Boston: Osgood, 1878.
Drift from Two Shores. Boston: Houghton, Osgood, 1878.
An Heiress of Red Dog and Other Tales. London: Chatto & Windus, 1879.
The Twins of Table Mountain and Other Stories. Boston: Houghton, Osgood, 1879.
Jeff Brigg's Love Story and Other Sketches. London: Chatto & Windus, 1880.
Flip and Found at Blazing Star. Boston and New York: Houghton Mifflin, 1882.
In the Carquinez Woods. London: Longmans, Green, 1883.
On the Frontier. Boston and New York: Houghton Mifflin, 1884.
By Shore and Sedge. Boston and New York: Houghton Mifflin, 1885.
Maruja. Boston and New York: Houghton Mifflin, 1885.
Snow-bound at Eagles. Boston and New York: Houghton Mifflin, 1886.
The Queen of the Pirate Isle. Boston and New York: Houghton Mifflin, 1887.
The Crusade of the Excelsior. Boston and New York: Houghton Mifflin, 1887.
Frontier Stories. Boston and New York: Houghton Mifflin, 1887.

A Millionaire of Rough-and-Ready and Devil's Ford. Boston and New York: Houghton Mifflin, 1887.

The Argonauts of North Liberty. Boston and New York: Houghton Mifflin, 1888.

A Phyllis of the Sierras and A Drift from Redwood Camp. Boston and New York: Houghton Mifflin, 1888.

Cressy. Boston and New York: Houghton Mifflin, 1889.

The Heritage of Dedlow Marsh and Other Tales. Boston and New York: Houghton Mifflin, 1889.

A Waif of the Plains. Boston and New York: Houghton Mifflin, 1890.

A Ward of the Golden Gate. Boston and New York: Houghton Mifflin, 1890.

A Sappho of Green Springs and Other Stories. Boston and New York: Houghton Mifflin, 1891.

A First Family of Tasajara. Boston and New York: Houghton Mifflin, 1892.

Colonel Starbottle's Client and Some Other People. Boston and New York: Houghton Mifflin, 1892.

Sally Dows and Other Stories. Boston and New York: Houghton Mifflin, 1893.

Susy: A Story of the Plains. Boston and New York: Houghton Mifflin, 1893.

The Bell-Ringer of Angels and Other Stories. Boston and New York: Houghton Mifflin, 1894.

A Protégée of Jack Hamlin's and Other Stories. Boston and New York: Houghton Mifflin, 1894.

Clarence. Boston and New York: Houghton Mifflin, 1895.

In a Hollow of the Hills. Boston and New York: Houghton Mifflin, 1895.

Barker's Luck and Other Stories. Boston and New York: Houghton Mifflin, 1896.

Three Partners. Boston and New York: Houghton Mifflin, 1897.

Stories in Light and Shadow. Boston and New York: Houghton Mifflin, 1898.

Tales of Trail and Town. Boston and New York: Houghton Mifflin, 1898.

Mr. Jack Hamlin's Mediation and Other Stories. Boston and New York: Houghton Mifflin, 1899.

From Sand Hill to Pine. Boston and New York: Houghton Mifflin, 1900.

Under the Redwoods. Boston and New York: Houghton Mifflin, 1901.

Openings in the Old Trail. Boston and New York: Houghton Mifflin, 1902.

Trent's Trust and Other Stories. Boston and New York: Houghton Mifflin, 1903.

Miscellaneous Editions

Ah Sin: A Dramatic Work. Ed. by Frederick Anderson. San Francisco: Book Club of California, 1961. (With Mark Twain.)

Bret Harte: Representative Selections. Ed. with an introduction by Joseph B. Harrison. New York: American Book Co., 1941.

Bret Harte: Stories of the Early West. Foreword by Walter Van Tilburg Clark. New York: Platt & Munk, 1964.

Bret Harte's California. Ed. with an introduction by Gary Scharnhorst. Albuquerque: University of New Mexico Press, 1990.

The Lectures of Bret Harte. Ed. by Charles Meeker Kozlay. Brooklyn: privately printed, 1909.

The Outcasts of Poker Flat and Other Tales. Introduction by Wallace Stegner. New York: New American Library, 1961.

"The Rise of the 'Short Story.'" *Cornhill Magazine,* NS 7 (July 1899):1–8.

Sketches of the Sixties. 2d ed. Ed. by John Howell. San Francisco: Howell, 1927, 1–114.

Stories and Poems and Other Uncollected Writings. Ed. by Charles Meeker Kozlay. Boston and New York: Houghton Mifflin, 1914.

Sue. London: Greening & Co. Ltd., 1902. (With T. Edgar Pemberton.)

Letters

Atkinson, F. G. "Bret Harte: A New Letter." *Notes & Queries,* 21 (January 1974):28–29.

Booth, Bradford A. "Bret Harte Goes East: Some Unpublished Letters." *American Literature,* 19 (January 1948):318–35.

————. "Unpublished Letters of Bret Harte." *American Literature,* 16 (May 1944):131–42.

Cevasco, G. A., and Richard Harmond. "Bret Harte to Robert Roosevelt on *Two Men of Sandy Bar*: A Newly Discovered Letter." *American Literary Realism,* 21 (Fall 1988):58–62.

Harte, Geoffrey Bret, ed. *The Letters of Bret Harte.* Boston: Houghton Mifflin, 1926.

Murphy, Brenda, and George Monteiro. "The Unpublished Letters of Bret Harte to John Hay." *American Literary Realism,* 12 (Spring 1979):77–110.

Interviews

Dam, Henry J. W. "A Morning with Bret Harte." *McClure's,* 4 (December 1894):38–50.

Haskell, Mabel Percy. "Bret Harte in London." *San Francisco Examiner,* 12 February 1893, 17:4–5.

Sharp, Luke. "Francis Bret Harte: Two Interviews with Him on Somewhat Dissimilar Lines." *Idler,* 1 (April 1892):301–11.

SECONDARY SOURCES

Bibliographies

Barrett, Linda Diz. *Bret Harte: A Reference Guide*. Boston: G. K. Hall, 1980. An annotated list of approximately 2,350 reviews and comments about Harte published between 1865 and 1977.

Gaer, Joseph. *Bret Harte: Bibliography and Biographical Data*. California Literary Research Project, 1935; rpt. New York: Burt Franklin, 1968. Basically a table of contents to the Standard Library Edition of Harte's writings with some original places of periodical publication cited. Woefully incomplete, but the only published bibliography that even presumes to trace the first appearances of Harte's later work.

Stewart, George R. "A Bibliography of the Writings of Bret Harte in the Magazines and Newspapers of California 1857–1871." *University of California Publications in English,* 3 (1933):119–70. A reasonably complete listing of Harte's early publications, specifically in seven periodicals.

Books and Parts of Books

Brooks, Cleanth, and Robert Penn Warren. *Understanding Fiction*. 2d ed. New York: Appleton–Century–Crofts, 1959, 181–85. A brief critique of "Tennessee's Partner" as a mawkishly sentimental "story of a man's intense loyalty to his friend."

Duckett, Margaret. *Mark Twain and Bret Harte*. Norman: University of Oklahoma Press, 1964. A first-rate, fully-documented record of the friendship and feud between the two authors. Perhaps the outstanding achievement in Harte scholarship to date.

Hazeltine, Mayo W. *Chats About Books, Poets, and Novelists*. New York: Scribner's, 1883, 287–99. A laudatory review of Harte at midcareer.

Heywood, J. C. *How They Strike Me, These Authors*. Philadelphia: J. B. Lippincott, 1877, 197–223. A contemporary comment on Harte as a humorist.

Mark Twain in Eruption. Ed. by Bernard DeVoto. New York and London: Harper & Brothers, 1940, 254–92. A celebrated outburst of scoria that has set the tone for most modern discussions of Harte's character.

Morrow, Patrick. *Bret Harte*. Boise, Idaho: Boise State College, 1972. Boise State College Western Writers Series Number 5. An adequate overview of Harte's career marred by occasional factual errors and an overemphasis on his literary criticism.

———. *Bret Harte: Literary Critic*. Bowling Green, Ohio: Popular Press, 1979. Analyzes Harte's critical beliefs and practices with particular reference to his "Condensed Novels" and *Overland Monthly* reviews.

————. "Bret Harte, Mark Twain, and the San Francisco Circle." In *A Literary History of the American West*. Fort Worth: Texas Christian University Press, 1987, 339–58. The sections of this essay devoted to Harte mostly summarize the essayist's earlier publications on the subject.

O'Connor, Richard. *Bret Harte: A Biography*. Boston and Toronto: Little, Brown, 1966. A useful, albeit derivative record of Harte's life largely based on Stewart's biography and Duckett's book above.

Pemberton, T. Edgar. *The Life of Bret Harte*. New York: Dodd, Mead, 1903. Hagiography of Harte by his friend and collaborator.

Quinn, Arthur Hobson. "Bret Harte and the Fiction of Moral Contrast." In *American Fiction: An Historical and Critical Survey*. New York and London: Appleton–Century Co., 1936, 232–42. An excellent biographical sketch and summary of Harte's major themes.

Stewart, George R. *Bret Harte: Argonaut and Exile*. Boston: Houghton Mifflin, 1931. The most reliable, if not quite the definitive, biography of Harte.

Walker, Franklin. *San Francisco's Literary Frontier*. New York: Knopf, 1939; rpt. Seattle: University of Washington Press, 1969, 64–69, 106–109, 126–32, 213–17, and passim. A fine account of Harte's early career in the context of the contemporary California literary climate.

Williams, Stanley T. *The Spanish Background of American Literature*. New Haven, Conn.: Yale University Press, 1955, vol. 2, 208–39 and passim. Considers Harte one of the eight "major interpreters in American literature of Spanish and Spanish–American cultures." In his tales of California life he "wove his fantasy of a golden world under the Spanish and Mexican governors."

Articles

Boggan, J. R. "The Regeneration of 'Roaring Camp.'" *Nineteenth Century Fiction*, 22 (December 1967):271–80. Suggests that the ironic narrator of "The Luck of Roaring Camp" does not speak in the voice of a Christian believer and that the men of the camp are *not* regenerated. A rejoinder to Brown's essay listed below.

Booth, Bradford A. "Mark Twain's Comments on Bret Harte's Stories." *American Literature*, 25 (January 1954):492–95. Prints Mark Twain's marginalia in his copy of *The Luck of Roaring Camp and Other Sketches* (1870).

Brown, Allen B. "The Christ Motif in 'The Luck of Roaring Camp.'" *Papers of the Michigan Academy of Science, Arts and Letters*, 46 (1961):629–33. Interprets the story in traditional terms as a Christian parable of redemption.

Buckland, Roscoe L. "Jack Hamlin: Bret Harte's Romantic Rogue." *Western American Literature*, 8 (Fall 1973):111–22. A useful taxonomy of the 20 tales in which the character Hamlin appears.

Burton, Linda. "For Better or Worse / Tennessee and His Partner: A New Approach to Bret Harte." *Arizona Quarterly*, 36 (Autumn 1980):211–16. Attempts, albeit unconvincingly, to explain the curious friendship of Tennessee and his partner in terms of a homosexual union.

Canby, Henry Seidel. "The Luck of Bret Harte." *Saturday Review of Literature*, 17 April 1926, 717–18. A review of Harte's *Letters* that, while granting his limitations, credits him with broad influence upon later writers.

Carranco, Lynwood. "Bret Harte in Union (1857–1860)." *California Historical Society Quarterly*, 45 (June 1966):99–112. A brief account of Harte's early years in Humboldt County, California.

Clark, George Peirce. "Mark Twain on Bret Harte: Selections from Two Unpublished Letters." *Journal of English and Germanic Philology*, 57 (April 1958):208–10. Excerpts two letters Twain wrote Howells in 1879 and 1903 that allude to Harte.

Conner, William F. "The Euchring of Tennessee: A Reexamination of Bret Harte's 'Tennessee's Partner.'" *Studies in Short Fiction*, 17 (Spring 1980): 113–20. Argues persuasively that Harte designed the tale to satirize sentimental conceptions of friendship by appearing to satisfy pious readers' expectations.

Duckett, Margaret. "Bret Harte and the Indians of Northern California." *Huntington Library Quarterly*, 18 (November 1954):59–83. Summarizes Harte's opposition, expressed in his early journalism and in such stories as "The Princess Bob and Her Friends," to the doctrine of manifest destiny and the policy of extermination.

————. "Bret Harte's Portrayal of Half-Breeds." *American Literature*, 25 (May 1953):193–212. An insightful essay about Harte's sympathetic portrayals of mixed-blood characters, especially in "A Pupil of Chestnut Ridge," "The Mermaid of Lighthouse Point," and "The Ancestors of Peter Atherly."

————. "Plain Language from Bret Harte." *Nineteenth Century Fiction*, 11 (March 1957):241–60. A cogent review of Harte's liberal attitude toward the Chinese in California and his satire of race prejudice in such works as "Plain Language from Truthful James."

————. "The 'Crusade' of a Nineteenth-Century Liberal." *Tennessee Studies in Literature*, 4 (1959):109–20. Perceptive analysis of Harte's novella *The Crusade of the Excelsior* as an anti-imperialist allegory modeled in part upon the career of William Walker.

Friedrich, Gerhard. "Bret Harte as a Source for James Joyce's 'The Dead.'" *Philological Quarterly*, 33 (October 1954):442–44. Identifies *Gabriel Conroy* as a potential source for Joyce's story.

Gardner, Joseph H. "Bret Harte and the Dickensian Mode in America." *Canadian Review of American Studies*, 2 (Fall 1971):89–101. A fine survey of reviews and critical studies published between 1870 and 1903 that com-

142   BRET HARTE

pare Harte to Dickens: a "test-case" for defining what Dickens seemed
to represent in Gilded Age America.

Gates, W. B. "Bret Harte and Shakespeare." *South Central Bulletin*, 20 (Winter
1960):29–33. A valuable taxonomy of the nearly 100 Shakespearean allusions in Harte's works.

Glover, Donald E. "A Reconsideration of Bret Harte's Later Works." *Western
American Literature*, 8 (Fall 1973):143–51. Pleads the case for Harte as a
talented storyteller even in his late, critically neglected fiction.

Hill, Hamlin. "Mark Twain and His Enemies." *Southern Review*, NS 4 (Spring
1968):520–23. A provocative comment on the sources of Mark Twain's
antipathy for Harte.

Hudson, Roy F. "The Contribution of Bret Harte to American Oratory." *Western American Literature*, 2 (Fall 1967):217–22. A superficial account
largely derived from Stewart's biography and Kozlay's edition of Harte's
lectures.

————. "From Poker Flat to Sandy Bar." *Pacific Historian*, 6 (August
1962):129–37. Places the original site of Poker Flat at O'Byrne's Ferry
in Tuolumne County and Sandy Bar on the Stanislaus River some 10
miles away.

————. "Roaring Camp Revisited." *Pacific Historian*, 5 (May 1961):69–76.
Places the original site of Roaring Camp at Quail Gulch on Horseshoe
Bend on the Stanislaus River.

Hutchison, E. R. "Harte's 'Tennessee's Partner,'" *Explicator*, 22 (October
1963):item 10. Defends the formal characteristics of Harte's story against
Brooks and Warren's charge of sentimentality.

Kolb, Harold H., Jr. "The Outcasts of Literary Flat: Bret Harte as Humorist."
American Literary Realism, 23 (Winter 1991):52–63. Argues persuasively
that Harte's enduring popularity is rooted in his ironic perspective,
which distinguishes his work from that of Mark Twain.

Lauterbach, Edward S. "Tom Hood Discovers Bret Harte." *American Literature*, 34 (May 1962):285–87. Summarizes Hood's allusions to Harte in
Fun, a British humor magazine, between 1869 and 1874.

Lewis, Ward B. "Bret Harte and Germany." *Revue de Littérature Comparee*, 54
(April–June 1980):213–24. A solid history, largely based on published
sources, of Harte's literary experience during his residence in Germany
between 1878 and 1880.

Loomis, C. Grant. "Bret Harte's Folklore." *Western Folklore*, 15 (January
1956):19–22. A brief and superficial listing of some folkloristic elements
in Harte's fiction, particularly those related to mining and gambling.

Luedtke, Luther S., and Patrick Morrow. "Bret Harte on Bayard Taylor: An
Unpublished Tribute." *Markham Review*, 3 (May 1973):101–105. Reviews Harte's infrequent associations with Taylor and prints (notwithstanding the misleading subtitle of the essay) an English translation of

the printed German translation of a tribute Harte wrote for a Berlin paper on the occasion of Taylor's death in 1878. The original MS, which has never been published, is located in the Alderman Library at the University of Virginia.

May, Charles E. "Bret Harte's 'Tennessee's Partner': The Reader Euchred." *South Dakota Review*, 15 (Spring 1977):109–17. Emphasizes Harte's sardonic humor and moral complexity in a revisionist reading of the story.

May, Ernest R. "Bret Harte and the *Overland Monthly*." *American Literature*, 22 (November 1950):260–71. An excellent history of Harte's editorship of the first 30 issues of the *Overland Monthly* between 1868 and 1870.

McKeithan, D. M. "Bret Harte's Yuba Bill Meets the Ingénue." *Mark Twain Journal*, 14 (Winter 1967–68):1–7. Largely a plot synopsis of "An Ingénue of the Sierras."

Morrow, Patrick. "Bret Harte and the Perils of Pop Poetry." *Journal of Popular Culture*, 13 (Spring 1980):476–82. Recapitulation of the publication history and reception of *Outcroppings* in 1865–66.

———. "Bret Harte, Popular Fiction, and the Local Color Movement." *Western American Literature*, 8 (Fall 1973):123–31. A brief review of Harte's role as a pioneer of local-color realism.

———. "Parody and Parable in Early Western Local Color Writing." *Journal of the West*, 19 (January 1980):9–16. Superficial, if sympathetic, summary of Harte's early career.

———. "The Predicament of Bret Harte." *American Literary Realism*, 5 (Summer 1972):181–88. A reasoned brief defending Harte's significance and place in the canon.

Murphy, Francis. "The End of a Friendship: Two Unpublished Letters from Twain to Howells About Bret Harte." *New England Quarterly*, 58 (March 1985):87–91. Prints two letters from 1877 in which Twain urges Howells to intervene with Rutherford B. Hayes to deny Harte a diplomatic post.

Oliver, Egbert S. "The Pig-Tailed China Boys Out West." *Western Humanities Review*, 12 (Spring 1958):175–77. A brief comment on Harte's sympathetic portrayal of Chinese characters in "Wan Lee, the Pagan."

Scheick, William J. "W. D. Howells to Bret Harte: A Missing Letter." *American Literary Realism*, 9 (Summer 1976):276–79. Prints a letter from 1874 in which Howells negotiates with Harte.

Scherting, Jack. "Bret Harte's Civil War Poems: Voice of the Majority." *Western American Literature*, 8 (Fall 1973):133–42. Evaluates Harte's Civil War poems as cultural documents that illustrate the attitudes of loyal Californians during the conflict.

Schroeder, Fred E. H. "The Development of the Super-ego on the American Frontier." *Soundings*, 57 (Summer 1974):189–205. A provocative Freudian reading of "The Luck of Roaring Camp."

Stewart, George R. "Bret Harte Upon Mark Twain in 1866." *American Literature,* 13 (November 1941):263–64. Reprints a paragraph about Twain that Harte wrote for the *Springfield Republican* early in his career.

Thomas, Jeffrey F. "Bret Harte and the Power of Sex." *Western American Literature,* 8 (Fall 1973):91–109. An excellent essay on an original subject: eroticism in Harte's fiction, a topic he treated repeatedly with surprising realism, especially in his late work.

Timpe, Eugene F. "Bret Harte's German Public." *Jahrbuch für Amerikastudien,* 10 (1965):215–20. A valuable history of Harte's reception in Germany, especially between 1872 and 1884.

Williams, Stanley T. "Ambrose Bierce and Bret Harte." *American Literature,* 17 (May 1945):179–80. Prints a brief note Bierce wrote Harte circa 1870.

Young, James Harvey. "Anna Dickinson, Mark Twain, and Bret Harte." *Pennsylvania Magazine of History and Biography,* 76 (January 1952):39–46. A brief history of Dickinson's friendship with Harte.

Index

The Author

Gary Scharnhorst is Professor of English at the University of New Mexico. He is the author of two earlier TUSAS volumes, *Horatio Alger, Jr.* (1980) and *Charlotte Perkins Gilman* (1985), as well as other books and articles on Alger, Gilman, Nathaniel Hawthorne, Henry David Thoreau, Emily Dickinson, W. D. Howells, Henry James, Mark Twain, Owen Wister, and F. Scott Fitzgerald in journals such as *American Literature, American Quarterly, American Transcendental Quarterly, New England Quarterly, Arizona Quarterly, Studies in the American Renaissance, Studies in Short Fiction,* and *Modern Fiction Studies.* He also serves as coeditor of *American Literary Realism.* A recipient of research grants from the National Endowment for the Humanities and Radcliffe College, he has held two Fulbright teaching fellowships in West Germany, at Stuttgart University (1978–79) and Heidelberg University (1985–86).

.